We Used To Be Wives

We Used To Be Wives

~

Divorce Unveiled Through Poetry

JANE BUTKIN ROTH
EDITOR

2002 · FITHIAN PRESS
SANTA BARBARA, CALIFORNIA

Printed in the United States of America

Cover art by Jackie Jasina Schaefer

Published by Fithian Press
A division of Daniel and Daniel, Publishers, Inc.
Post Office Box 1525
Santa Barbara, CA 93102
www.danielpublishing.com

Second printing

LIBRARY OF CONGRESS CATALOGING-IN-PUBLICATION DATA
We used to be wives : divorce unveiled through poetry / [compiled] by
Jane Butkin Roth.
p. cm.
ISBN 1-56474-390-X (pbk. : alk. paper)
1. Divorce—Poetry. 2. American poetry—Women authors.
3. Divorced women—Poetry. I. Roth, Jane Butkin
PS595.D58 W4 2002
811.008'0355—dc21
2001007558

Dedicated to

my children
Adam, Jill, and Emily
my greatest blessings

~

also dedicated to

Sarah Bernice Butkin
and to the memory of Morris Butkin
my parents
whose marriage convinced me
that lasting love
is a possibility

Acknowledgments of personal thanks

A special thanks to Christopher Woods, my mentor and cherished friend, without whose constant encouragement and humor over the past five years, this manuscript would never have found its way out of my head and into print.

Heartfelt gratitude to all of the contributors for sharing their words, their lives.

My deep appreciation to John Daniel at Fithian Press for wholeheartedly embracing this anthology, for his assistance in the final shaping of the book, and for being such a gem to work with.

Thank you to a wonderful group of writers, teachers, friends, and family for their time, suggestions, and support, including Celeste Bowman, Jim Buttler, Ginny Connors, John Fox, Ken Kopel, Barry Pulaski, Adam Roth, Emily Roth, Jill Roth, Gail Storey, Jack Thomas, and Linda Woods. Thanks also to my friends who helped pull me through the darkest days of my divorce and continue to stand by me, especially Eva Ackerman, Ann Maltz, Kathy and Stephen Parven, Risa Streusand, Rosie Quiller, and Linda and Peter Zweig.

Special thanks to Marty Braniff and Karen Krakower for their belief in this book and its potential for healing, for their generosity in time, their excellent advice, and for giving 110 percent whenever I needed them at any hour of any day. Most of all, I thank them for enriching my life with their friendship.

In grateful remembrance of my friend, Susie Bowers, writing sister, confidante, and a soulmate who passionately supported me in the creation of this anthology.

My gratitude for crossing paths with Jackie Schaefer, the delightful artist whose vision captured the right mood for the book's cover.

I thank Rabbi Roy Walter for his wisdom, guidance—and a poem—during my most challenging time of transition.

A special thank you to Robert Butkin—my brother, my hero—and to Nancy Herzog—my sister, my best friend—for their enthusiasm for this project, for their loyalty, and for their confidence in me and my dreams. I owe them a world of gratitude.

Thank you, Patti Leeman, my sixth-grade English teacher, for asking to buy the first copy.

Finally, special thanks to Adam Roth, my son, for giving this book its title.

Contents

61

Children of Divorce

Poverty and Void

Ugliness

Dormant Strength

Supporting Roles

The Patterns Continue

The Past in Present Light

Introduction

The Naming of Things: The Roots of *We Used To Be Wives*

Seven years ago I ended my sixteen-year marriage to the father of my three children. Seven years ago I began to write with new urgency, fueled by a tremendous, unquenchable need to name my feelings in the wake of divorce, even when what I felt was more lost and nameless than cogent or concrete. My marriage had suffered a tedious death over a span of years; it seemed logical that my divorce would be an anticlimactic ending, a formalized cutting of ties to a union from which I already felt estranged. As it happened, I was surprised by its impact, which hit me not all at once or in predictable ways, but in increments, at unexpected moments.

As I walked new ground, searching for a foothold in an altered life, the aftermath of my divorce took on many personalities, which appeared out of nowhere, like uninvited guests. Some barged in all at once; some held more power on different days; others popped their heads in for attention at any given moment. Some were welcomed visitors: liberation; stimulation; wonder; resolution. Peace. Some were obstructive intruders: sadness; guilt; confusion; uncertainty. Panic. I yelled at them, begged them to leave: *Get out of here. Let me get on with my life. Move forward.*

They wouldn't listen. I wrestled with them. They kept winning.

These ill-behaved, runaway emotions took over, then demanded that I write them. So I did. And I listened. Powerful, even dictatorial before I wrote them, they overwhelmed me and held me hostage. As I wrote, they seemed larger than life. Monstrous. But after a while, seeing on paper my impressions of that strange time in my life—exploring, questioning, and naming the things I felt—turned them into something else. Something newly tangible and simultaneously distant.

Two distinct changes occurred. First, the emotions became less powerful. When I got them down, let them have their say, and gave up the fight against them, I discovered we could coexist. I could look at them, examine them, and begin to make sense of the ways my life was changing, without feeling that the emotions were swallowing me whole, rendering me immobile.

The second and more positive effect was that the release of my emotional energy to pen and paper brought an acceptance of myself as a woman who houses the capacity for vulnerability, cynicism, defeat, and despair equally to her propensity for joy, passion, conviction, and hope. I could see myself more comfortably as one who is at once frightened, clueless, capable of undignified thought and act, as well as intuitive, independent, directed, and brave.

Ah, Sweet Acceptance.

I don't suggest that I no longer need improvement, or that self-acceptance is an easy goal, or even one that is truly achievable as an endpoint. I think of it more as a quarrelsome travel companion: challenging to have along, sometimes annoying as hell, but better than traveling alone. Giving ourselves permission to express all aspects of our experience—the negative, unflattering, embarrassing emotions alongside those that convey our strength—keeps us from getting in our own way, stuck in the pain and numbness that are an essential, but challenging and perplexing, part of our healing. It is a point to move *from,* but not by sheer will—or denial. It's a sticky place in which we must stay stuck…for a while. Acknowledging those times when we feel the most powerless and broken is a step *towards* regaining our power. As we reassemble the fragmented pieces of our lives and identities, we discover untapped strengths that eventually guide us towards action and responsibility. In divorce, many of us embark on a journey that was forced on us; others choose its difficult path. Writing, for many of us, is an essential tool for navigating our way. It's how we explore and comprehend our lives. To express our experience—to honor *how* we experience in the face of divorce—is an enabling, productive, and therapeutic thing. There's no shame in it.

Some months before my divorce was final, I enrolled in a writing class under the instruction of an inspiring teacher, and it was his unwavering belief in his students that kept me focused at an unfocused time. In his class grew the roots for this anthology. My poems inevitably turned, for better or worse, to divorce, as I reflected on my years of marriage, the home I had shared with my husband, our young children who would forever be changed by my unilateral decision effecting the destruction of our household and family as we'd known it.

Encouraged by my teacher and classmates who suggested my writings might warrant a bigger project, one that could appeal to a wider authorship and readership of women who had experienced or contemplated divorce, I placed a single ad in a writers' marketing magazine. My only requirement was that the authors must have experienced divorce first-hand at one time or another, because I wanted the poems to come from the authenticity of experience. I had not imagined that one ad would elicit several thousand responses, many from well-published authors with long lists of accomplishments, book publications, and awards. Many were accompanied by notes of appreciation for my efforts towards a book that would at last present the divorce experience in a creative format currently missing from the shelves of books on divorce. As I began the task of reading the submissions, it became apparent that, although each person's situation and reasons for divorce are unique, there are universal pains, regrets, challenges, and stages of divorce. Thus began *We Used To Be Wives* and my privilege in the role of caretaker of these poems from more than seventy authors.

As I shared the poems with writers and friends—with women who were divorced and women who weren't, with men, with adult children of divorced parents—their feedback taught me that not only is the writing about divorce therapeutic, there is also healing and comfort in the reading. Some felt the poems expressed their own experiences, which validated and consoled them; others said they gave them insight into family members' or friends' experiences. Still others said it relieved them *not* to be able to relate to some of the poems, reminding them that no matter how difficult their own situations, there is always someone who has it worse.

Thoroughly Modern Divorce: Call It What It Is

The new millennium finds women in a stimulating, electrifying era, a time of vast opportunities never before at our disposal. Women can shine in every capacity in every field, in positions previously afforded only to men. We can participate fully to help define, shape, and change our world. With new possibilities come new choices, which positively affect our marriages *and* divorces. No longer do we have to define ourselves so narrowly in terms of a wife's more traditional and antiquated role. And more and more, women no longer have to stay in loveless marriages for financial security.

During this grand time of opportunity, the divorce rate is so high that it's almost as commonplace as marriage. Divorce is glossed over as the norm, rather than viewed as a disruptive, jolting trauma; the experience is minimized, ho-hummed, barely registering on the societal pain scale. There is a lack of entitlement to mourn. Divorce is no longer the stigma; lamenting it is. It's as if we are told, or tell ourselves, that there are so many other things a woman can be, aside from a wife, that she shouldn't spend so much time whining. Besides, everyone and her sister have been divorced, so what's the big story here? Two dichotomous symptoms of our current times, the exponential divorce rate and expanding options for women, work against us in our healing process after divorce.

The changes that the ordeal of divorce demands of us are no less momentous than those incurred by any other trauma, including untimely death. Our modern mentality impedes recovery. Both women and men, no matter how successful, or in what field, still value and seek a partnership or marriage; and the longing to find that person with whom we can share our lives in an enriching, evolving, respectful climate of love, is a timeless one. That core need is as intrinsic to human nature in the twenty-first century as it was in the 1800s. Granted, modern times shape our visions of ideal marriage; most women are less interested in playing Harriet to an outdated Ozzie, or the proverbial princess locked in a dark tower, awaiting rescue by her prince. But the basic yearning for partnership is alive and well, and when that union we deem as our chosen, most special relationship falls short and crumbles, it is no less traumatic simply because we find ourselves in a time that trivializes the impact of such a loss.

Call it what it is. Divorce is death. Loss. Failure. The final acceptance of that failure is staggering; the challenge of reckoning with its long-term effects, stunning. Divorce is uprooting. Disorienting. Saddening. Maddening. We are entitled to grieve it, explore it, and seek understanding and awareness from it. Let us not negate who we are by downplaying our deepest needs and desires just because opportunities for participating in the dynamics of the greater world are more accessible than ever to women, as they should be.

A Message of Gratitude: To the Contributors

With humor, heart, wisdom, and attitude, this collection validates our diverse experiences—without editing the rougher parts of ourselves—as we forge new lives after divorce. I took lessons from my contributors, some of whom shared revealing, raw truths, some quite unflattering about the way they behaved or felt during a specific time in their divorce process.

There are poems of deep rage and vengeance. This doesn't mean I advocate revenge or that the women who wrote those poems are, or remain, spiteful, embittered man-haters. Rather, their poems are an essential expression of yet another stage one may go through in divorce. Scary. Alarming. Shocking, perhaps. But they are part of their truth; part of the journey towards something better.

There are poems of paralyzing sorrow, including one in which the author shares a time when she contemplated suicide. The author bewails her despondency, and then affirms her conscious decision to live, as she remembers the ordinary pleasures in her daily life. This kind of duality explicit in many of the poems gives the writings their richness and power, rather than perpetuating a simplistic image of women as victimized or weakened at the hands of the villains.

There are no clear villains, and by extension, no victims. Regardless of how the gavel falls, or the decree is written, there are no winners, either. We all lose in divorce. What loss could be more monumental than that final shredding of shared hopes and dreams, the breaking of vows, the coming apart of our most significant union, the one to which we entrusted our hearts and declared to the world to value above all others, to protect until our deaths?

The spectrum of poems included herein honors our capacity for a full range of emotion, some of it extreme, provoked by anguish and loss. They demonstrate our ability to suffer, endure, survive and thrive. These poems, collectively, are testimony to the resiliency of our spirits.

I am grateful to the contributors, not only for their talents as poets, but also for their courage to reveal so much of themselves, at times in less than favorable light. They give us permission to be a little more truthful and a whole lot braver. We can say ourselves out loud, as these contributors have done so honestly and beautifully. We can reveal our flaws and explore the overwhelming, halting sorrow that brings us to our knees, the undignified thoughts of vindictiveness, the patterns of unhealthy behavior we often repeat. We can examine our periods of incapacity and bewilderment, knowing these are stages in healing, which sometimes rise to the surface on the journey through grief.

We plod along, fumble, fall. And then we get up. We assess our priorities and access our strengths. We reclaim ourselves, newly empowered. We flourish in our new lives while honoring all the things that shape us along the way. We are on a path, making better choices, while remembering no road is straight or without occasional rough terrain.

To the Reader:
On That Twisted Road From Here to There

No matter who makes the first appointment with his or her lawyer, or who finally pulls the plug, extinguishing all potential for a shared life; regardless if the decision is a mutual one, amicably agreed upon, or how polished your pre-and-post-divorce manners; no matter how wide the arms of support of friends, family, therapists, and clergy—divorce is a journey each person must navigate alone. It is my hope that this book will be helpful on your solitary path and that each of you finds solace in these poems. From the threshold of your deepest pain and loss, as you leap into the darkness of uncharted territory, may these writings encourage you to honor your Self, the many dimensions that comprise Who You Are: wondrous, complex, and capable. As you rebuild your life and set out on your path towards self-discovery, I wish you unexpected joys. I invite you into this collection with the following poem.

From the Threshold

Do not ask your sadness
to go quietly,
leave her tears at the door,
not to enter.

Do not make grief
crawl away
until she begs forgiveness,
or force rage into a corner
hiding, like some child
you're ashamed of.

Give Sorrow a song,
even when she moans.
When she screams,
give Rage her part to play.
Hand Loss a microphone,
especially when she's voiceless.

Then marry—
    pain to joy; anger to awe; loss to hope.
Bless them. Let them live together.

And when you can, wrap your arms around them.
Let them all hold hands in your house.

—Jane Butkin Roth

We
Used
To Be
Wives

Falling Before Divorce

"Trying to write down how love empties itself from a house,
how a view changes, how the sign for infinity turns
into a noose for a couple."

—Dina Ben-Lev

Mary Kennan Herbert

August Alarums

Cicada choirs: this swelling sound,
this buzz announces the conclusion of lives,
perhaps yours or mine. These heavy blossoms
and curled leaves are lush with summer,
yet they cannot fool me: I see leaves
with brown edges, drooping flags—
some cannot keep up.

Along this shore the swells are the same,
pregnant and super slo-mo, muted, opaque.
A layer of memories lies between me
and the sea; Virgo air is heavy with sadness.
The shrinks are away, shorebirds are packing
their bags. I am thinking about autumn,
even at high noon here in paradise.

Things are not clear. Shadows are longer.
I cover my ears to block out your music.
Your swimsuit lies in the corner of the closet,
in damp darkness—already forgotten.
The brilliance of June mornings
is barely recalled on these afternoons
of dull gold, not quite in focus.

MARY HAZZARD

Suppose

you build a village
on the attic floor
near the tracks of a
Lionel train.
Set houses in rows,
tiny trees,
the church with the
steeple,
a bit of mirror.
Arrange cows and sheep,
out of scale
but what you need.

The train runs and comes back.

The pattern grows too easy;
not, after all, what you wanted.
You wonder
how it would be—
only to try—
if you moved the track three inches over.
You do. You pull the switch.

The engine
        starts, striking sparks, hits a
                house it didn't expect, which hits
another. A wagon is up-ended, cows scattered, trees
        tossed, engine on its side at last,
                wheels whirling.

This is not what you meant.

Barbara Hendryson

What You Long To Return To

It is morning. Your coffee, roll
inundated with sweet jelly, are taken
in what I see is your need for silence.
Systematically shaved, suited up,
magnificent watch caught in the
dark hairs on your wrist, buzzed
with the brilliance that lies before you,
you move to the door. I wish,
just this once, you would turn
in my direction, be astonished by
what you see, by what you long
to return to. But you step
from the house to the world:
what you look at, constantly,
through the evening windows;
where you ache to be.

MARGE PIERCY

A story wet as tears

Remember the princess who kissed the frog
so he became a prince? At first they danced
all weekend, toasted each other in the morning
with coffee, with champagne at night
and always with kisses. Perhaps it was
in bed after the first year had ground
around she noticed he had become cold
with her. She had to sleep
with heating pad and down comforter.
His manner grew increasingly chilly
and damp when she entered a room.
He spent his time in water sports,
hydroponics, working on his insect
collection.

Then in the third year
when she said to him one day, my dearest,
are you taking your vitamins daily,
you look quite green, he leaped
away from her.

Finally on their
fifth anniversary she confronted him.
"My precious, don't you love me any
more?" He replied, "Rivet. Rivet."
Though courtship turns frogs into princes,
marriage turns them quietly back.

Francine Witte

Falling

We drove past a field of strawberries
darkened by too much rain and the ending
of June. They hung like medals on the chests
of old soldiers, tired stems stooping
toward the ground. You stopped the car
and led me to them. I felt their white-
flecked skins, and inhaled the scent
of approaching sleep. You said anything
on its slow way down will make promises,
which is why strawberries hang on,
their puckered shells empty
as parting lovers and a last
long drive on a country road
where even strawberries eventually fall,
clear a field, make room for a setting sun.

SHARON LYNN BEAR

The Card You Gave Me on Our Wedding Day

The card you gave me on our wedding day
Used to sit on my nightstand

It spoke of your love for me
How I complete your life

It sat on my nightstand
For over two years.

It has been subjected to the elements
The heating and cooling of the air

It has become bent over time
And can no longer stand on its own.

I had to put it in the drawer
Where it is now silent

Where it no longer sits
Only sleeps.

MARY HAZZARD

Untrue

I gave him a
promise
but then he gave it back

and for five
years it lay good as gold
in a blue velvet box
with the glass beads from Venice
and the turquoise beads from Taos
and all the unsuccessful gifts
and the peace symbols

until I asked
him to take
it again

All right he said
but don't write a damn poem
about it

I said I wouldn't

Kathi Hennessy

Morning, After Dreaming

A young woman shivers
alone at her kitchen table.
Indifferent to time's passage,
she abstracts herself from
the real, worrying
the memory of last
night's dream in which
her husband died and she
did not feel sad, but vaguely
relieved. Bothered by this,
fingers absently skimming
a bruised forearm, she
wonders for the first time
where she left her self.

Sharon Lynn Bear

Unraveling

The fabric of my marriage is unraveling
I am not surprised
I chose the wrong cloth.

I love the fabrics with texture,
    the nubs and slubs of life
I love the fabrics with bright colors,
    exotic, even erotic, designs.

But mother always told me
    "Choose something practical
    Something which won't show the dirt.
    It may not be as exciting
    But it will last."

Yes, the cloth has lasted
But it remains unworn
Its textures and colors are flat.

It sits in the closet
Unraveling.

Mary Kennan Herbert

At a Family Reunion

a sacrament yet the clan gathers in discomfort
here are snippets

guarded conversations
memories wrapped in a hideous foil

slings and arrows   ethnic jokes
fraternal barbs in profusion

tenderness well hidden   love restrained
passion denied

what else shall I list
in this beach-stained album

full of our many photographs
your children and mine

line them all up according to size and age
dress them all in souvenir tee-shirts

so I can use up rolls of film
get everybody's mug for eternity   don't move

here you will be in a supersize print
I share the negatives with one and all

I will send prints to all on the family tree
who knows where those pictures may be eventually

by the time you read this
half of us are divorced and half of us are dead

there are no guarantees
I do not love you   but here we are

doing this family thing   knowing the uselessness
and importance of these chronicles

Leilani Wright

Bird's Nest

"For there is hope of a tree, if it be cut down, that it will sprout again, and that the tender branch thereof will not cease."

Job 14:7

You are not crazy,
you argue, and then he's won
because the moment you lose sight
of the tree, start defending
that soft planet behind the eyes,
doubt grows in his mind.
He has that knowledge
as a weapon, not that you're insane,
or even unbalanced,
but have seen a shrink,
wondered a time or two aloud—
enough that the garden debate
is reduced to this hot button.

It doesn't help that a number
of relatives have been put away
in institutions and parks,
leading through the family tree,
like ants that march
toward a lesion leaking sap,
to that one branch,
where you are a leaf.

We argue about the orange tree,
and how far back, if at all, to cut
one limb that had cracked
in rainless wind and thunder.
Prop it up, he says
from behind his beard,
and splint the fractured wood.
No, you say, *this branch is unsound*
and must be pruned
at the break.

Hummingbirds had built a nest here,
entrusted their family
to the breezy tap and shush
dappling the shade where he stands,
doubting your evidence.
Today, three tiny eggs
are white dots on the lawn.
There's grit between your teeth
as you study how the branch
droops to earth,
heavy with small, green fruit,
half born and yet dying.

Tammy Vitale

Changes

Sometime during the night
she became a kangaroo.
In the mirror in the morning
she did not find this
any odder than
most waking moments
even though she blinked
three times to clear
her eyes instead of the usual
twice.
At breakfast her daughter
admired her newly acquired
boxing skills demonstrated
by knocking flies right
out of the air and
her son inquired
as to the convenience
of her pouch for carrying
tools and treasures. Her
husband thought her tail
magnificent. She found
running for the bus such
fun, she
passed the bus, bounded
all the way to work by
herself and still had her
breath. Skipping her
lunchtime workout, she gossiped

in the park with squirrels
about the best way to care for fur and
the benefits of stored body
fat in winter. At dinner
she left a list of food
hanging on the fridge
and sat by the pond to draw
frogs. Her family wandered be-
tween the cabinets and stove,
lost, and called to her, "You're
different." She answered back,
"Yes, I've changed."

Diane Lutovich

Curious Artifacts

Notice the tension between man and woman,
the anger hiding
behind their smiles,
imagine the dozens of times they've promised never
to see each other, never use
the other's body to keep out darkness.

See how they look
at the child, this glue stick,
a place to focus
their eyes

The father's arm appears
to encircle his wife's shoulder,
look closely,
it doesn't touch,
all mirrors
baby's body is out of the picture,
she looks down, maybe at her toes—
how long before they can walk
her away

Add twenty years to their faces,
jowls heavy with missed chances,
middles thickening—gravity and mistakes

The sharp featured child
no longer stares at her toes,
is no longer in their pictures.

The picture fades
between plastic pages.

Marge Piercy

Never-never

Missing is a pain
in everyplace
making a toothache
out of a day.
But to miss something
that never was:
the longest guilt
the regret that comes down
like a fine ash
year after year
is the shadow of what
we did not dare.
All the days that go out
like neglected cigarettes,
the days that dribble away.
How often does love strike?
We turn into ghosts
loitering outside doorways
we imagined entering.
In the lover's room
the floor creaks,
dust sifts from the ceiling,
the golden bed has been hauled away
by the dealer
in unused dreams.

Margaret Kaufman

The New Kitchen

I.

Low-E, they call it, and "safety" glass:
our choice, the kind of window you can't see through
or the kind that is clear—either
protects from heat loss, cold mornings.
There is security in opaque glass, you say.

What your face shows when I look at us
side by side in those snapshots someone took,
what your eyes tell me
as they stare into her camera:
how unhappy you are in this life.

II.

I was the one who wanted this,
as if new ovens would warm us, new cabinets
hold what ruins we have stored against our time.

He comes home late, showers at once.
Suspicion hangs like leaking gas
in this room that will be so nice,
orderly, empty.

III.

The moon rises in the new windows,
shines at the far end of the room
through clear glass.

Everything is back to normal,
the painters' drop cloths swept away
and underneath, after all, our customary
chairs, patient as elephants.

We take up old positions
reading by the fireplace as before.
Irritable when I fail to hear
something he's asked,
he thinks we're in the same room.

Discovery and Decision

"First he said he didn't want to be married to me anymore, then he bought me a hat—"

—Diane Lutovich

Frances Downing Hunter

Turbulence

Not earth shaking news, no plane crashed after
lights flashed warnings to occupants of an ordered
universe. No buckled seats fell to ocean's floor
holding faceless bodies safely in place.

Place and face flew yesterday at 10:00 P.M.
when he said, *I don't want to be married.*

Keddy Ann Outlaw

Things I Don't Want To Share With Him Anymore

Towels
telephones
the refrigerator
bed sheets
coffee mugs
car keys

Car insurance
garbage cans
the oven
the salt and pepper

Mirrors
forks knives
spoons
plates and bowls

Sunlight in the yard
dark nights
lazy afternoons
aspirin
ice cubes

Christmas
lawn chairs
toothpaste
my best cooking
my worst cooking

Yard work
home maintenance
my headaches
my heartaches
anger
love
sex
or taxes

the rest of my life

Diane Lutovich

Hatted

First he said he didn't want to be married to me anymore,
then he bought me a hat—black felt, brim wide, turned out
like wings, and a crown,
slightly creased, snugged my head.
We admired me in mirrors, painted glass,
others' faces, even eyes, hiding
behind brims.

It was at a street fair, warm, end of summer,
lights everywhere—like
India heavy with strings of bulbs—turned night
to a slightly sinister day; I strutted, the way
you do when you know people admire you—one man
applauded, another shouted, "Eva Le Gallienne!"

We held hands, ate mocha chip ice cream,
later beer and hot dogs, continued to hold hands.
On that windless night, the hat stuck, like a great disguise.

That night we made love with all the lights on,
as if we were still at the street fair or in India,
as if everything wouldn't be different tomorrow. The last thing
I removed was the hat.

MARGARET KAUFMAN

Waking

Morning light over the sill.
She extends one wooden arm,
pushes her hair back,
bends her neck— from her breasts
the scent of bay leaves.

Finally it is happening—
she lifts the hem of her gown,
steps out of their bed,
over the carpet
down the stairs,
and lifts the latch.

Outside, in stronger light,
she examines her hands,
regards her bare feet: green everywhere.
Your imagination, he'd say.

No! in every step,
she breaks into a run holding her hands
before her, flexing the fingers,
opening, closing, opening.

Deborah Miller Rothschild

First Time Around

Too weak not enough character her mother said but she did it *her* way
and said yes because she didn't want to hurt his feelings and didn't
know where her life was going and agreed to a wedding his mother
planned even though the last thing she wanted to do when the Big
Day came was walk down the aisle and marry that hung-over boy
sporting a bad haircut and a dark blue suit but the organ was playing
and she was standing with her father at the back of the church and
everyone was looking at them so she married him anyway and had a
miserable time at the reception and spent a dismal two days in a
rainy beach town at a second rate motel fantasizing about old
boyfriends before returning to their apartment over a garage and a
summer job with the telephone company that she quit in the fall to
return to college which she never finished because he accepted a
job in another town and they had to move so she went to work and
earned more money than he did but took a back seat and after she
had her first child she became a full-time-mom and made homes in
houses that suited him and lived in places he wanted to go and
entertained his friends and one night after a dinner party went to
bed and awoke by herself in a too still house and quietly walked
down the hall to the living room where candles were burning and he
and his best friend were naked on the carpet doing things she never
imagined men did together and when they didn't see her she went
back to bed and buried that scene deep in her head to continue life
as his wife and had another child and followed him across the
country to escape his interfering family when something deep
within her fought hard to get out yet all she could say was I don't
want to hurt you and I know that you need me but I don't think you
love me anyway I don't love you so she moved him out on Valentine's
Day and went back to her house where she phoned her mother and
said *Well I guess you were right*.

Joyce La Mers

Cocktails for Two

We met in the Roosevelt lounge
and ordered drinks
as if to celebrate.
I'd come from work.
You'd been somewhere
for days
without an explanation,
though clean shirts left your drawers
when home was empty.
And then your call.
We had to talk, you said.

You talked, self-conscious,
solemn. *Lugubrious*, I thought.
I saw you'd taken off the ring
that matched my own,
a pair you'd bought
just three short weeks before
to mark our anniversary,
measuring my finger
while I slept.

Outside, late sun blared red
across a cratered landscape
pocked with palm trees.
I found my keys and drove.

At home, two kids
waiting for dinner.

Henny Wenkart

On Waking From a Nap

Drowsily I stretch into the pleasure of your voice
On the telephone in the other room
A pleasure I do not take for granted these days.
I'm sitting here waiting for what's her name
That is what I hear you saying.
Dear God in heaven!

Oh, good, you say, *you bought it... it comes 20 x 60, or 30 x 60?*
But we're getting 20 x 60, right?
WE?
Well, you got a good buy because you took it without the glass.

You run through a list of names, people you'll call next
I know most of those names
But whoever you are talking to KNOWS THEM ALL!
I'll be home tomorrow, you say
But, I think dazed, you are home now!

Quickly then, before the other person can hang up,
You say into the phone *I love you.*

That's when all the walls collapsed.

Joan Jobe Smith

Begin the Beguine

Fourth of July, 1965, his own personal
Independence Day, after he left me alone
with three kids, one a baby, rent a week
overdue, no milk or bread in the place,
I lay in bed all night plotting my suicide
just like every woman abandoned there's
ever been, not knowing then about Sylvia,
not that poetry would've mattered.

I planned on gas, too. This: Me in the car.
In the garage. Doors closed. Ignition.
Exhaust. Sweet dreams. The note
reading: "I can't go on. I loved him so."
An hour before dawn was when I'd do it.
Kiss my sleeping kids goodbye. Phone
their grandmother: Come and get them.

Then I'd sneak quietly outside, down
the stairs past the bougainvillea, neatly
dressed, my hair combed, I'd even
shower first and brush my teeth, the
starlight express of sad night speeding me
to begin the beguine, but come the
ultramarine of pre-sunrise, my tears
dried up, a neighbor's alarm clock went off,
someone simmered coffee next door,
birds sang, my kids woke and I
wanted to live. It was only then that
I remembered: I didn't have a car:
He'd driven away in it.

KAREN ETHELSDATTAR

This Is a Poem That Says Lady Macbeth's Head Was in the Wrong Place Because It Wasn't Her Own

This is a poem about giving and giving and giving
to a man who takes and takes and takes
and grudges giving back and no thanks

This isn't just a poem about no thanks for dinners and clean linen
and supermarket lines and walking the floor with babies at night:

    This is a poem about no thanks even for driving nails,
    plastering walls, hauling lumber up the stairs

This is a poem about a man's anger that dinner was late
because of a poem:

    This is a poem that says next time he can get his own

This is a poem about going it (at last) alone

    About learning to fix a refrigerator plug
    and three broken windows
    and bellow a drunk bum out of the hall

    About swatting full-grown roaches
    with the flat of my hand

This is a poem that says I value Myself and My body
                My children and My poems

                more than any man's arms.

Barbara DeCesare

Gimme an A

Gimme an A
Gimme a big red A

Pin it to my ass so you can see me going.

Gimme an A
Gimme a big red A
to go with my
big red lips

my big red lips
kissing the man I love

the man I love
ain't you.

Francine Witte

Perception

That evening, our last, though I couldn't have
known, I must have struck that pose all lovers
take when the ground fails and they hang
from a split in the earth, when they know

they've been mid-air from the start.
You told me the trick is perception,
that instead of loss, this was opportunity
and that pulling the background forward changes

the shape of a thing. I thought of those pictures
of goblets that turn into faces, or flat
shaded circles that swell into spheres.
And I'm not the first who, seeing disaster, mistook it

for love. Watching you leave, your thin shadow stretching
behind you, I suddenly wondered which one was real.
I thought how heavy the sun must be, sinking
each evening into the sky, when, in fact,
it really hadn't moved an inch.

MARY E. O'DELL

Dorothy, You'll Have To Find Your Own Way Home

It's time I took myself to some far place.
Futility of casting about
to make a rift
a shift
a jolt in this mad, technicolor world
comes boiling up like scum on a kettle stirred
by that old sister of the west.

But though the forest's gloomy here,
its demon trees are only cronies of the dark
and not the dark itself.
The gremlins, vicious monkeys, are within us daylight folks,
working their wills
in our livers,
our hearts or brains
or in some follicle clutching eyelash root.
We feed them as we might parasites
not knowingly
willingly
but feed them, still.

And learning this,
I draw red, shiny slippers
on a page within my magic book.
I cannot conjure up the icons needed
to grant wisdom, heart or courage;
I make these shoes for myself.
And now I draw my own slim ankles
sprouting upward from them.

This Wizard's proved to be a midget.
Soon I will dismount this merry basket,
click my heels,
disappear into the celluloid crowd.

Celeste Bowman

I Married a Four-Door Ford

He rolled up the drive, an unwaxed gray exterior
boasting a nondescript hood ornament.
His spark plugs fired when he got a load of me,
my interior velvety and lush to the touch.
I was at least a Mazda, maybe a Peugeot.
He, a four-door Ford at best.

He'd been traded in twice. Me, I was
barely broken in, still smelled new.
He pulled up beside me, his engine, used
to idling, revved more than safe for an
older model. I was tired of the racetrack,
but thought he was running on higher octane
than he was.

I signed the license and shared a garage,
him, stuck in neutral, his tan upholstery
aging, cracking, collecting dust. Me up on blocks,
my starter disconnected. I was on empty so long,
I forgot what a full tank felt like.

I left a message under his wipers to blow it out
his pipes. Got myself some new wheels and
recharged my battery. A friendly mechanic, a
frisky 'Vette, oiled me up and fine-tuned me,
and I was back on the freeway of love
before my four-door Ford knew
he'd crashed and burned.

Finding the Way Out

"...odds and ends of broken dreams, broken unions."

—Jane Aharoni Berman

Ann B. Knox

I Divorce You

It's simple. Say it three times
in the presence of witnesses, if
their presence troubles, practice
on the porch, say it aloud to the hawk,
whisper it in the round holes of carpenter bees,
press your lips against the pine's bark,
say it and breathe the smell of resin, say it
to the hand you hold over your mouth,
say it to the mirror, note your eyes
and teach them to repeat the words.

When you have it perfectly, knock
on the library door and walk in. He'll
turn, but you won't see his face for the light
behind him, only the way his hand holds
open the book, how age has thickened his knuckles,
how his body leans toward you hunched like a target.
The words crouch ready in your throat, but remember,
once they are sprung, you can count on nothing.

Barbara Daniels

Finding the Way Out

after a line by Martha McFerren

More women have done this
than you can imagine, driven cars
'til they're out of gas, stepped
onto bare ground, walked

from field to field collecting stones,
slept in the blonde grass. I know
I could live like an animal, let
knives darken in their wooden cases,

dust thicken on smeared mahogany,
dishwater curdle in the cold sink.
I've got my story: It's a form
of getting out, a long flat highway

or a short escape—a dream
in the morning before the alarm.
Even a hummingbird falls asleep,
slows the constant motor of her heart,

lets trumpet flowers bloom
in her trembling eyes. Truly gone
is harder, but it can be done.
Women get away on a daily basis.

You just don't see them in the flagrant
rain, the solemn fog that starts the day.
They pick up their pocketbooks, open doors,
pin red flowers in their gleaming hair.

Elisavietta Ritchie

Clearing the Path

My husband gave up shoveling snow
at forty-five because, he claimed,
that's when heart attacks begin.

Since it snowed regardless, I,
mere forty, took the shovel, dug.
Now fifty, still it falls on me

to clean the walk. He's gone on
to warmer climes and younger loves
who will, I guess, keep shoveling for him.

In other seasons here, I sweep
plum petals or magnolia cones
to clear the way for heartier loves.

Jane Butkin Roth

Breaking Bread

You took the house, I took the dining table, and we split our children right down the middle—although it's hard to divide three so they come out even.... And so it went, plate by plate, undoing what was left of our lives together. It was not an unpleasant morning; we were always at our best with a project. Later, I heard you worried I might have sneaked an extra Pyrex.

Now you come in, uninvited, and stare at my walls where paintings, which used to be ours, are mine. I can see your discomfort. Though I gave you all your first choices, you say, "I'll trade you the Gorman for the Fairchild, or the two Mortensens for the Miro." But there comes a time to stop passing things across the lines.

Your main irritation is at the breadmaking machine on my crowded counter-top—such a modern convenience, so easy, so fast. You remember when its blade gave out, letting us down like a broken promise. You tell me you would like it, that you would fix it. But I won't give it up and I won't fix it, and I see how crazy it still makes you for me to let things go. You were always so efficient. Even before the breadmaker fell apart, it was mostly hype, as it popped out its tiny, misshapen or too-perfect loaf, its aroma barely a hint....

Before the machine came into my life, I used to braid my own loaf: a wondrous work of art. I loved to work the dough all day; it held me close to the house as I waited for the yeast to bring life. I was kneading...punching...waiting in stages until the smell filled the house, until we were both done—the loaf and I—golden, glistening, and proud.

My broken breadmaker takes up too much space now. It's quite lifeless and useless. But I keep it. Today, when you leave, I open the top and peer in, surprised. It takes only one tear to make a tinny sound falling on a dead blade; one tear to mark a time when our home was filled with the fragrance of bread in the oven, when everyone had his place, and I still wanted, more than anything, to set our table.

Adrian Blevins

Mid-Divorce Weather Report

Last night I tried to say some things about the things that don't or can't get said. Maybe that's why this morning's hollandaise curdled up like it thought I was foolish and had to knot its brow. Since I didn't know why or why not, I ate it over eggs and bacon. I was the broken bishop surveying from his bloody skirts the king's cremated kingdom. Before you and I put on our knapsacks, what did we speak of? In that final moment, why couldn't I close my eyes and put my fingers to your mouth? And why couldn't you know what to say? So why couldn't we talk of what would become of us once the store-keeper hovered the CLOSED sign in her stupid yellow window? I don't know what you'll think of me after I am dead. Sweetheart, I know so little now. For instance: why can't you hear those insects? They sound to me like children telling lies. One day soon, I'm going to give corruption up. I'll tell our boys fate's a slow star spinning toward them from the sun. I'll show them they've got this life and not one other. But already the sky's too ardent in their little sundial faces. Honey, it's true they fling themselves so far into me they almost split my spine. *Mom,* they say, *we've lost our goddamned hats. Hey, Mom,* they say, *we think it's going to rain.*

Lynn Asch

The Divorce

A single swallow rises between you
and me. A single syllable holds there
in my throat each time I feel the
ancient pull toward you. The magnetic
wonder of heart song flows like a hidden
spring between us. I won't erase it
with my tears, nor will you with a
thousand distractions. We are joined
at the root in the underground
place nobody knows except us
in our deep bones.

Now the trick is in the throat—
in the newly forming flap there
which decides *yes* or *no*, keep or let go.
As more and more of you slides out of me,
breathing eases, my heart expands
to fill my chest, to fill the room.
I can allow now, allow for breakage,
go with less fear into life
knowing I have survived death
in surviving you.

Now I know where the edges of my life
are, the continually shifting shadows
between me and not-me
between me and you
between birth and death.
I spread from dawn to the deepest
midnight, from here to the farthest
galaxy, from yesterday to forever
with my heart as sentinel,
navigator and guide.

Linda Goodman Robiner

Six Year Divorce

Like Sisyphus, I keep pushing the boulder
up the mountain. It rolls down again

as soon as I near the top. Divorce seems
about to be granted, and then more delays.

The unstoppable playing out of conflicts
from a marriage. Tantalus, at least, was given

something to eat. Of course, every moment
he reached for food or water, they were gone.

Jane Aharoni Berman

Rabbinical Court, October 16, 1994

I let nothing go, never throw
away what has passed.
Like the beads from Sina's necklace
that snapped—ping!—in the corridor
of the Rabbinate
on the day of Susie's divorce.
How we waited—Susie, Yoram, the lawyers—I was the witness—
for the mysteries within
to reach their finale.
The scribe—I think—was writing
the divorce decree—eleven lines, Nuri had said
on the day of our divorce.
I was wearing Sina's beads, fingering them perhaps
when all of a sudden they snapped,
and ping-ponged on the floor
along the paneling
under the scarred wooden benches.
With a gasp we scurried
to pick them up, cull them
like treasures.
Susie and Yoram clinked them
into my palm.
Each time we spied one we cried,
Here's another!
Yoram's lank body split in two
like a popsicle stick as he stooped
to gently grasp the bead,
Susie scooped them up in one swift motion.
Their duty done, they returned to their
divorce perusal, anger in their eyes,
sitting on the scarred benches, Yoram's long legs crossed,
ankle on knee—Susie, hunched, one foot
tapping.

Only I remained, my fist
brimming over with beads
like a fountain of tin.
Still, my eye kept lighting on strays
lurking in corners, or right at my feet.
That was the greatest surprise—to see
in plain view—where I had looked a thousand times—
new beads appear.
It happened again and again—as if air made
solid shapes, protoplasm, out of nothing
to tease me.
Even when the door opened
and the young clerk, his red sidelocks dangling
like tassels,
came out to call them—
even as they entered the judges' sanctum, even as I waited
for it to be over—
a stray bead tantalized me—air
metamorphosizing into matter—
into kneeling, plucking it, placing it
in my overflowing palm.
Where to put these treasures, wayward bits
of a divorcing life?
Dumped in a zippered pouch,
a handbag compartment
Where they lie to this day, unseen, unsifted,
tucked away, random
like on that divorce day.
Perhaps even now
beads are coalescing out of thin air in that corridor
at the Rabbinate—
odds and ends of broken dreams, broken unions.

Tina Kelley

July 1995

Here is the sound of this month:
the laying down of windchimes,
their flat staccato discord,
the solid reality of divorce.

If a marriage ends in the woods
does it make a sound? I look around
quizzically. Shouldn't something more
happen now? Was the union so weak
it can die this quietly? Where's
the gnashing of teeth, the shrieking,
the Greek chorus that stood at our wedding?

You broke my name.

Shouldn't it matter more somewhere?
Where's the garlic press? Oh! And the calculator?
And all our unspent playful time?
And the man I asked for comfort?
I briefly meant to bring this ache to him,
but remember he caused it.

These are sadnesses I had tried on before.

Barbara DeCesare

Dog Years

This Three-Year Anniversary
is celebrated with paper and glass.
Glass comes first, smashing against the
freshly painted walls, the antique mirror rests in slivers
on the oak bureau and wood floor
(both with a lemony scent).

That Christmas you get
Stained Glass Lessons
for us to take together, in the city, somehow reasoning
cutting up
and changing the colors will help me see things differently. Instead
I build windows for the dog house.

Paper flies in. Smooth in fat envelopes,
brought by strangers, quickly signed.
Paper on my floors, hanging out my window,
noting the true terms of the marriage
with its new vows.

If we were lesser beings
it would be 21 years. I would never have
run out of gifts to give you.
A lick here and there,
prizes left on the stoop,
obedience
day in,
day out.

As it is the gifts are many.
There are endless ways to cut
with paper and glass.
Endless.

Mary Kennan Herbert

A Beautiful Bowl

booty of divorce
this wooden bowl
still mine

still useless
on display now
in this invisible room

as if this were a museum
preserving art and life
carved of tropical wood

not politically correct
but beautiful
smooth to the touch

an unusual shape
slender oval for a finger
to follow

hollow   ancient female form
into which we tossed
not lettuce   but letters

from lawyers
until I took this bowl away
bearing it to safety

innocent bowl
gently carved
sanded by a dead artisan

an artist who does not
know this story
but knows about things

that can be held
close

Arlene L. Mandell

After the Decree

The woman hacked her way through the thicket wearing heavy work gloves, wielding sturdy pruning shears, straining toward the small stream which gurgled unseen. Starlings screeched from their high outposts.

First she tried to bend the arching branches of thorn bushes away, but they whipped back with cruel efficiency, scratching her cheek and drawing blood. She began slashing them low with her left hand, whacking them lower with the dead limb in her right hand.

Technically, these were no longer her woods. Deer and raccoons, their claims older than any deed, had left their prints on the creek's muddy edges. Behind, her house loomed brown and expensive with meters whirring and overdue bills spilling off the once polished counters.

Clip and whack, clip and whack. Bending nearly double, she saw mossy rocks and stray sunbeams. An inch-long thorn pierced her glove into her palm. She stripped the glove, sucked the red from the wound. Adultery. Bankruptcy. Foreclosure.

She tore at the thicket, found a hole big enough for a small animal, chopped some more until she could crawl through to a flat rock. Her cheek stung and her palm ached where it had been punctured. Now she tilted her face toward the sun, dangled her legs over a creek clogged with a hundred years of debris. She dipped her hand in the chill water and tasted its sweetness.

Ann B. Knox

Clematis

We do not touch to say goodbye. You carry
an armful of books to the car and come back
for your duffel. Air stirs as you pass,
you do not look at me, but old habits of discourse
stay, small courtesies—I proffer coffee,
you comment on the pink clematis by the door
that blooms this year for the first time.
These exchanges cannot camouflage a parting.

I watch for some sign, a gesture of your hand,
a bend toward as we speak of the children, car,
mail to be forwarded. I want to forgive you,
forgive myself, be forgiven. Without looking back,
you brush the vine and a few petals scatter,
as if your going were a simple matter.

Still Life

"There is the weight of every shadow in your house,
piling up in rooms like dust or palpable regret."

—Diane Pinkley

Diane Pinkley

Still Life

The varied shades of gray,
like ash, tell a story
as intricate and many-hued
as fire's.
There is, for instance
the shade your sweat socks
attain after many washings
and runnings
on lonely morning paths
in the space echoing
after arguments.
There is the predictable
metal of the Michigan
sky to stare through with
the phone receiver still in hand,
buzzing like an insect.
There is the weight
of every shadow in your house,
piling up in rooms like dust
or palpable regret.
The gray of morning teeth and
breath, the middle-aged hair
of marriage,
the gray of every calendar day
and what it will never hold,
not now.

Lucinda Grey

You Feel It

in the long hum of the pipe
after the water's off,
in the rush of the fan left turning
all night on the porch, miles away
from anyone who loves you.
You wait in the wheeze of a bus
for someone to get off.

Then at dawn when you still
haven't fallen asleep,
there's the wail of the morning train
announcing arrival, departure.

Henny Wenkart

Broken

My mainspring is broken
I try to hold it together with my fingers
Still renew my subscription to *The New Yorker*
Look at the cover
    not at the stories
    or even the jokes
Here is a copy four years old
Dated the weekend you first spoke the work *divorce*
It is folded open to the middle of
A long article that I was
                                        reading

NANCY MEANS WRIGHT

Hunger

Snow eases off to flurries and
three young deer plunge
down out of the heaped woods

to the steps of my glassed-in
porch to nibble the frosty
scrubs. They stare in, bold

as children demanding milk
and pie in the sanctuary of friends;
their eyes are hungry-brown,

their ears laid back like women
on soft quilts. They stamp
in dazzling white while I am quiet

as black ice, they haven't
caught my scent through glass.
A year ago I watched you

from a doorway: hands moving
slowly up her ivory silk sleeves;
her head flung back to feel

your lips on her flushed neck.
Filled with self-pity, for I
was cold out there in the late

winter wind—I knocked. You
coughed. And we wheel about
and flee, back up to woods, our

tails like blown snow, our tracks
already overlain with thick
slow flakes; our bellies, empty.

JOANNE McCARTHY

The Lover Returns

at night he comes back
the dead lover rises
out of the grave where I've laid him
he slides by my shutters
insinuates himself under my door

he gathers himself over my pillow
and his cold flesh congeals in my bed
all night I lie wrapped in his faithless embrace
at night, only at night, he comes back

BARBARA HENDRYSON

Poem Written Between Midnight and Morning

This night, the moon releases
its least light. It is in the dark
sector we call northwest, the night zone.
From that direction, a familiar pair—

the man blonde, the woman having long
dark hair—practice their slow
expected walk past the walls
of my house. I see how

they touch each other; how the soft
cord of their love passes between them.
Later, I dream of someone caressing
my face, caressing the sleep-

flattened strands of my hair.
I wake crying for my aunt—the one
who loved me, dead twenty-five years—
thinking I'd die if I could be with her.

Anne Wilson

Unresolved

For a long time
after I'd learned
to live alone
again,
I drove past
lighted windows
of other people's
houses,
remembering
what it was like
to belong—
remembering the feeling
of home, shared
like a crocheted afghan.
I don't know
when one gets past the shaking,
the feeling of having dropped
into a well;
I don't know when terror ends,
or the longing
for a caress.

Flights of wild geese
across the twilight sky
unnerve me,
They are so purposeful.
I have been trying to heal
for seven years,
and I am *still*
driving past
lighted windows
of other
people's
houses.

Celeste Bowman

Rituals

It's not the new delights
you taught me,
flavors foreign to me,
that I miss most.

It's the old pleasures,
my special rituals
I shared with you, unwisely,
that have lost their charm for me,
a woman walking a solitary path
once again.

Immersion in my baptism
of oils, herbs, and English ivy,
a goblet of rich rosé beside me
a book of poems in damp hands,
and mellow music keeping time
with the flickering flames
of white vanilla candles.

My calico cat curled carefully
on the top step of the tub,
purring softly, staring down,
blinking her pleasure at
my quiet presence.
Once my carefully guarded gift
for myself at the end of arduous days,
now the loneliest parts
of living my life.

I act them out
because I must.
But I hurry, relieved
to slip between well-worn flowered sheets
and sink quickly and gratefully
into the vacant land of slumber
where everyone else
is as alone as I.

Barbara Daniels

Mark on a Mirror

A woman who used to start her days walking
from room to room emptying ash trays
lives now in a single room.

At night, her former house rises around her,
roof bent beneath the drill-marked sky.
People are near, supper in the oven.

Whose dog is this, nosing her stockinged leg?
She wakes from the repeated dream of slanted light
sorting through dust motes by a front window,

of dragging on an insubstantial cigarette.
She remembers a handprint on a mirror, mark
of a child trying to reach into another world.

The moon drops a glamorous silver coat across her bed.
Who will guard the woman's step, secure the clasp
of pearls at the back of her neck, balance her

on the turning ball of the world, her feet
like sweaty sisters in their sheer suits?
Can the moon protect her from blindness,

from staring tirelessly at the sea, the water improbably
forgetful? Will the moon lift her from the trench
of herself, hand her her broken umbrella?

Anne Lusby-Denham

After the Divorce

So this is the life
you now lead:
the curtains always drawn,
the air is stale,
a banana, which has become
a blackened shriveled husk,
sits on your desk.

I am glad to no longer
live in this place.

Yet there are days
when the phone
doesn't ring.
The only sound
is the whirring
of the fan
and the beating
of my heart.

REBECCA McCLANAHAN

Knowing How My Suns Die

We argued all night
and into morning
which I called *next*
but you called simply *morning*.
No such things as endings, you said.
Everything is round, repeats itself,
so when you see a bird
disappear into the west
if you sit in that place
long enough, watchful,
you will see the same bird
emerge in the east,
like the sun.

Speaking of birds, I interrupted.
You call them free
but if you're right
they are caught
in their closet of blue
doomed forever to move their wings,
never stopping, not even to mate.
And back to suns, I continued.
I have always believed
every sun is new,
birthed red in the east each morning,
stretching its life across the sky
to die in the west that night.
I have always believed what I see.

Then you called me Columbus,
threw back your head
and laughed my ignorance to the ceiling
where I said it falls
to the carpet to die
but you said it lives, reverberating,
bouncing back, floor to ceiling
to floor, always alive
in the spaces I cannot reach with my hands.
No, I argued, shaking my head.
I have always believed what I see.

So when you left
I cried, *Don't go,*
knowing how my suns die.
I watched you turn, and the laughter
you threw over your shoulder
I prayed would bounce from you
to me to you.
And I have sat in this place
so long. Wanting to be so wrong.
I sit still, try to feel
the dizziness there must be
if it's true
that we spin back
like your one sun,
the one you swear always returns.

Andrena Zawinski

Trying To Raise the Dead

"...we either forgive one another who we really are or not."
—Ralph Angel from "Love's That Simple"

I want you to say it   my name   and slowly
not fast as you read my note here   bent
characters that click   tick   in a pesky
night clock   I want to hear it   my name
haunt the stairs tonight in thin whispers
of wind trembling in   I want my name
to rattle your tongue with I'm sorry
I didn't mean to   I won't   not ever again
I didn't know what I was doing out there
in the drunken moon inside-out wrong

I want to hear my name fix itself upon
the bruised swell of this up all night
cried too deep   half sleep hurt   I could
forgive you anything   if I would hear you
say it   so I won't forget myself
in the dark here   in the fall air stiffening
into the tap   clack   of bare twigs against
the raised window glass   say it   so I won't
die alone inside tonight   my hands bloody
kneading this heart back to life.

Children of Divorce

"Assure them it is not their fault, that they are loved, that no one is to blame."

—Joyce La Mers

Susan R. Norton

Divorce Papers Scald My Hand

A yellow highlighted space bellows for my signature.
I coax eyes up from the burning document.
Scan my living room, hoping for a last reprieve.

My *Anthology of American Poets*
calms me with its presence.
Then I notice
his *Black's Law Dictionary*,
half reclining next to it.

Pushing up against both,
my daughter's *Where the Wild Things Are*,
struggling to hold the two together.

Sheila Bender

After We Collected Treasures From the Beach and Forests

My children play outside our house,
water running from the garden hose, a path
no wider than the ones they made for me
dragging kelp across the sand.

Children of my love of growing up, how do
I tell you your father and I must part?

Do I say, "Look at the surf broken sand dollars
left on our porch. Notice how we value remnants
of what once was whole?"

I touch the cones of Douglas Fir we brought
from the forests, bracts shaped like tails of mice
who ran up the tallest trees trying to hide from fire.

I think of you when you nap, hair wisps of smoke
against the amber linings of your sleeping bags.

Daughter, do you remember how you woke once
and told me you slit yourself open and bled
until a fairy came with magic dust and a wand
to heal your cut and teach you how to fly?

Son, when we walk behind the house in the alley
looking for garden snails on the underside of leaves
that hang over the fences, do you notice dandelions and sheep's
sorrel thriving, making it possible for other plants to grow?

Lucinda Grey

The Province of Fathers

Those evenings our daughter
hurled herself from the sofa
when she heard your footsteps,
you always caught her, though
you couldn't have seen her
perching there, ready
to cast herself into trust.

I'm trying to understand
the province of fathers,
what turns their bodies
into jungle gyms,
their shoes into dance floors.

I can see my own father
pushing my swing in the park,
running under it to lift me higher.
Later when screech owls called,
he'd carry me nodding to the car,
the odor of smoke in his shirt.

No wonder you stayed
long after you wanted to go,
long after there was anything
to stay for.

Susanne R. Bowers

Daughters

The horses were still marching
on her rug
when the moving van arrived,
and the people,
rubber dollhouse people,
lying face down
everywhere.
There must have been a storm,
a tornado.
She locked her bedroom door,
wouldn't let us in.

Her older sister
disappeared.

It was raining.

Linda Malnack

Tell Them

for Meagan

When you get to your father's
land, Van Diemen's Land,
tell them I didn't abandon love
at first.

I shielded you, sheltered
you, chopping wood in the rain;
I built fires, doused fevers, waiting
for your father's

return. Tell them I couldn't find time
to write—didn't know what to say—
that the house was robbed two times
in three days.

The thieves took all but hope
hidden in a tin under the sink.

Tell them about the night you turned
four. He finally came, calling names,
kicking the flimsy door to a tangle
in the moonlight.

Tell them my heart stopped
when the spit hit my face. His rage
stung my ears and hung with the echo
of your crying in the cold, dark

air under the apple trees. Tell them
you're all that's left.

Veva Dianne Lawson

Cold War

The Maginot Line follows the contours of the driveway.
The defenses are in place around the forget-me-nots,
meticulously arranged, carefully maintained,
    burying the blame.

The tower guards are on constant alert
searching the road for the scheduled assault.
Adversaries approach with the sound of the bell.
    When the door opens

at Checkpoint Charlie, the opposing force is there
grinning, well armed. "Daddy!" troops shout as
they rush into noisy, jostling formation.
    The trade-off begins.

Permission is granted through forced smiles
for this weekend furlough, with step-
mother, an alien family, a new brother,
    an other home.

They leave behind solitude in a house
suddenly too large. Always the whispered
retreat at the weekly prisoner exchange.
    Then come back to me.

Joyce La Mers

Telling the Children

It is important to say it right.
Choose words that will not
shatter self-esteem.
Assure them it is not their fault,
that they are loved,
that no one is to blame.

Inspire them with the joy
of facing changes.
Explain how all the pieces
will be neatly arranged
into a bright tomorrow
where all will thrive.

Let your face show
you have no tears or anger.
Tell them that love
will always be worth seeking
and often lasts forever.
Say it, say it, say it!

LAUREL SPEER

Things We Do Not Talk Of

We do not talk of the possibility one of my children
might die or be killed, prompting a call from my
unregretted ex-husband.
Wouldn't that be the only reason he'd call—
to tell me one of the children was lying on a slab
waiting his transmission of news?
But wait a minute, those children are all grown
and out on their own.
It doesn't matter.
These are the worst parts and we say let every day
be inconsequential rather than take away the few
things that keep our walls standing.

Lucinda Grey

I Watch Our Daughter for a Cue

And though the river forked
some time ago, one current running
over rock, the other over sand,
it's the same water she navigates
in her small boat, passing under
falls, shooting over rapids,
all our lives searching
for cove after blessed cove.

Poverty and Void

"But already I was on welfare, accepting slights and
innuendoes, brutal barters of collateral,
unwisely traded in the dark."

—Martha Everhart

Elisavietta Ritchie

After Long Absence, Mail Call

Each envelope brings threats:

one will cut the water off by noon,
a second, douse the lights, stop time,
another, disconnect the sewer pipe.

No more utility in my utilities:
every card in my Monopoly
leads straight to jail.

The only heat left is on me.
The bank warns foreclosure,
dispossession of my car.

American Express and MasterCard
shine plastic countenances full
of usury and menace.

No more safety in numbers
nor bulls in the marketplace.
And all my memberships have lapsed.

Patricia Lantay

No Earthly Paradise

Dawn seeps through the transom
under which I slumber
on a gym mat—
this makeshift pad
that makes one realize
a bed is a bed.
I want to leave
a note saying
I have had enough:
just this morning
the minister's wife

left two quarts of milk
and one loaf of bread
on the doorstep.
Unrehearsed for the role
of parish dole
something in me rebels.
I want to describe the face
of a wound that is the world
but too old to play the child
I look into the face
of my own child curled

in the crook of my elbow.
Her sleep is gauze
to hood my angry blood.
The iron door of poverty
opens as with a lion's roar.
You come in, hiding news
behind maverick eyes.
With reassuring tugs
I pry disaster from you
and live to rue my craft
You recite a numeral history…

the old car is totaled,
the rent overdue, the food low,
you are unemployed and no,
I won't consider moving again
except to the windowsill
that is bare as an altar.
I hear strange voices
and the tinkle of glasses
drifting past cages
intended as fire escapes
and come to know

the meaning of drift.
Their timbre is civilized;
not the raw scream
that climbs my throat,
clutching it like the tooth
of some rare Gargosaurus.
My hands, cuffed with age,
grow cold and wet with tears.
It has taken all this time
to tell you that love can pale
on a diet of dimes.

Martha Everhart

Half the Debt

When I said the word *divorce*,
he said, *You'll inherit half the debt*.
But already I was on welfare,
accepting slights and innuendoes,
brutal barters of collateral,
unwisely traded in the dark.

There was the time I tripped and fell
when pregnant with my first child.
He laughed and called me clumsy, then
later invited loyal friends to party
during twenty hours of labor
when he never said *I love you*.

You are weak, his explanation
for my morning sickness.
When I vomited, he sneered.
On Mother's Day he told me
I was ugly, truly ugly,
in my pregnant condition.
He counted on forgiveness,
so he bought expensive baubles
on birthdays and at Christmas.
All his friends could see that
he was a fine and loving husband,
and later a good father
who'd always make an entrance
at the children's birthday parties.

When the kids were sick or needed stitches
he had pressing obligations
at his company, which prevailed
as the True God of all days.
Attending church was different.
He'd never miss a service
to make important contacts that
could help his growing business.

My friends were always useless,
not at all like his compadres,
who agreed that every bad wife
would inherit half the debt.
While we women had their babies,
they stood in darkened hallways
and drank the best of liquor
to toast the coming generation.

Jane Butkin Roth

Faulty Design

I used to think
once we filled it up,
we would find our lives there.
Once we had more.
More furniture; more paintings;
more imported rugs; sculptures.

But there was too much greed in the design.
Our house had her own hungry mouth to feed.

She gobbled up
our inadequate possessions,
dwarfed everything.
Ravenous, insatiable.
We kept busy, collecting.

We nurtured our hunger
and hers, too great to feed.

We carefully stacked
dreams,
like deserted
chairs
piled high
on top of
emptiness
atop
pettiness
upon
void,

creating an illusion
that something was growing.

Elisavietta Ritchie

Savings and Thrift

I buy clothes second-hand,
haunt Goodwill for plates,
yard sales for chairs,
rent ramshackle houses,
invest in used cars.
My lovers also
have seen better days.
But what bargains I find…

Ugliness

"Same sad trailing, same silver ending—
the dish ran away with the spoon."

—Linda Malnack

Henny Wenkart

Comfort

Any woman I put in your place, you cry out to extend me this comfort,
Will be inferior to you.
All, all the ones I consider, you promise in desperation,
    all your inferiors!

With that and twenty-five cents
I can make a local phone call.
Waking alone before day what should I recite
For my comfort?

An inferior head now rests in his armpit
An inferior smell scents his bathroom
And on his shower rod
A pair of inferior panties?

Hours from now, in fresh sunlight,
An inferior woman's tongue will part his lips awake

Tania Rochelle

The Replacement

For months I've imagined brass
and polish, sharp edges—
a food critic, maybe,
or a stripper—someone
agnostic enough to tolerate
an indifferent lover, reluctant
father, petulant payer of bills;
and all that time, she's just
got to get to class.
Ten years younger, she shakes
her long brown hair
from her clueless face,
asks if I want my husband back.
She tells me she wouldn't *compete*
as if it were a gift,
more lead crystal
to leach slow poison
into my daily cocktail.
So fresh I could bite her,
this girl, twenty-one, still
smelling of grass and Kool-Aid,
is asking permission.
But I'm not her mother—
to care if she runs
with a pencil in one hand,
a fork in the other.
Let her keep her prize:

his glass-green eyes,
a gold-plated tongue
that ferrets out soft spots
where promises grow
wild as ivy, as fire
through parchment.
Searching her flat baby-blues
for ripples, the slight wave
that might suggest she stands a chance,
I see only a plain beauty,
hands in her pockets.

Pat Craig

A Letter to My Husband's Mistress

Dear Sheila,

At first I tried to not be angry with you. It was he who had strayed. You had no covenant with me. This was difficult. When he came home chortling at your naiveté at wearing a see-through blouse to work, boasting of how he had to counsel you and send you home to change, I grimaced. A grown man who could believe that a woman wore a see-through blouse with a see-through bra by accident! It was he whom I wished to brain with a baseball bat, though I could not see so tiny a target. It was he with whom I was angry. He was the one with the prick tied with a delicate pink ribbon, like a bull with a finger though his nose ring.

Later, when the children became so affected, I allowed myself to become angry with you. I see that I was wrong. I apologize. Now I want to press you to my breast and let you feel every joyous molecule of my body crying, "Thank you, thank you, oh thank you so very much!"

Please accept my heartfelt thanks. You have delivered me, rescued me, *saved me* is not even too strong a phrase. He could not give me what I needed, and I could not give him what he deserved, but with you—with you, he has gotten his just desserts.

Oh dear, that sounds a trifle bitchy, doesn't it? Well, forgive me. I'm tired and that really isn't what I meant to say. The real reason I'm writing you is that I wanted to tell you, sister to sister, that I sometimes lie awake at night, thinking of his return. What if you should find just the tiniest of flaws in him, a little snag or a loose button you hadn't noticed in the store? Canny shopper that you are, I know that this is unlikely. Still, I worry. What if he were to show up on the kitchen counter one morning, damaged merchandise returned to the point of sale? That simply would not do.

So, while we did not originally have a contract, you and I, I feel that we should draw one up now. I want to be clear and scrupulously fair. I've learned that you just can't be too careful in drawing up contracts. So, please, note the signs posted at the check-out counter. No Deposit. No Return. All Sales Are Final.

Sincerely yours,

His Ex

Dianalee Velie

Autopsy of the Heart

An autopsy of her heart
revealed words,
splintered words,
brittle, jagged sticks,
sentiments strangled on silence.
The examiner concluded
cupid inexplicably
pierced his valentine
until she bled over the lines
of devotion,
dripping along the curves
of compassion, coagulating,
shaping herself into
a sharpened point, a lance,
a weapon,

once designed to love,
now rebuilt for war.

Mary Kolada Scott

Dream House

Our house on the hill boasted
cathedral ceilings, picture windows
and three sets of French doors.
Spacious rooms which isolated us.

Our house became a gallery.
I hung paintings to cover holes
where my husband raged against plaster.
My son and I retreating to safer corners.

I ran out of wall space.
We moved to separate quarters.
The stripped house revealed battle scars
no amount of spackling could conceal.

In dreams I still inhabit these rooms,
walls blank as canvases, and doors open.
An ornamental tree scatters lavender tassels
on the front lawn each spring,
    drawing me out, out.

Dina Ben-Lev

How It Was

He was driving, he said, on the wrong
side of town, after bars closed,
because a man tires of right: right
clothes, right job, right way, and what he wants
is wrong. In the pitch of the dark,
in the street, a shape was waving at him.
And the car, he said, kind of drifted—
closer, he saw her pregnant belly
pressing against her dress. She wore
sneakers, but what got him, he said,
were the long, untied laces. Still waving,
she lost her balance and fell to her knees.
Should he have floored it and sped
heartlessly on, even if some sicko might find her?
Jesus, he just wanted to help. He rarely saw
such straight black hair, and he could see
she was young, yes, and definitely drunk
as she crawled to the door. Then the dome light
clicked on, and she was smiling beside him.
Eskimo maybe, or Indian, and he remembered
how wrong it was, his great-grandfathers,
their fathers, and all their guns. How natives
named it firewater because it made them burn.
Hell, all he wanted was to drive her home....
When he asked where that was,
she offered to suck him off.... The slut, what
was she trying to do, licking her lips,
then conking out in his car? Lucky for her
he wasn't the kind to grab her hair and go
at her throat with a knife from the glove box.
Lucky he wouldn't push up that dress and give her
what some men called real happiness,
In her shape it would've been easy.

She stunk like a bad experiment,
like lilacs and beer and something else.
With her eyes shut, her face was bearable,
he said, those black eyebrows, those lashes,
her long hair splayed over that great
mound of a stomach. Then it happened:
his hard-on, how all the wrong
beauty of her riled his blood.
He quickly unzipped—
but raised right for good, he said,
just jerked off on the fabric
around her swollen sphere.
Done, he drove to a faraway park,
and carried her, which wasn't easy,
to a spot in some bushes
where she'd likely be safe.
The cold was coming in on a wind,
so he shook out the car blanket,
and covered her, and stood there
a moment, bewildered—
Then he walked to his car and sped home,
to the warm bedroom he shared with his wife,
so he could finally get some sleep.

Amanda MacLeod

Daddy

"Why did you marry Daddy?" the children ask.
Each time I joke and tell them
another tale.

"Because I could beat him at cards," I say.
"Because he wouldn't leave my stoop."
Or, "Because someone had to."

But, to you, I'll tell the truth.

Because he raped me, and
I mistook it for love.

Mary E. O'Dell

American Theater of War

With you, I never knew the ravishment
of unpremeditation, never got the straight-out
hungry fuck,
mindless pound and slap, obsession driven home.

Choreographed to the last detail,
the classic climax was preceded by
setting of scene, costumes and make-up
checking out the props and lighting.

I took the script, prewritten
by your needy mind, and learned my lines.
Critiqued at each rehearsal, I honed them
to perfection.

With my acquiescence
I invested all my savings in the company,
bought great shares of shame
and vowed to outlive the director.

Susan R. Norton

Mid-life Fantasy Girl

It doesn't matter
that her past is checkered
like the red and white cloth
on our picnic table,
that her vocabulary is condensed
to two syllable phrases
like "Gee whiz" and "You know,"
that her best moves were learned
as an exotic dancer
in Cathedral City,
or that her favorite topic
of conversation
is herself.

All that matters is nothing
jiggles on her body,
except the diamond earrings
you gave her, her face
is stretched so tight
you could play jacks on it,
silicone breasts protrude
like the Washington Monument,
huge, pointed, rock hard,
and her age is one half yours.
It must be love!

Linda Malnack

Other Woman

Dish, dish,

the moon, soft
segment, raw
sentiment.

Spoon, spoon,

same sad trailing,
same silver
ending—

the dish ran away
with the spoon.

ANDRENA ZAWINSKI

Some Women, Take Heart

Some women learn to take it with a stiff
upper lip, stitched up tight, standing up,
right on the kisser, in the teeth, jaw wired,
bruised cheek swollen on a clip under
the eye. Some women take it flat on
their backs, slapped in a cast, choked,
roped in a free-kill-zone, run down out
on the road, statistics for *The Times*.

Some women take it into the heart-
land, run with what they own, new job, new
home, new name in balled fists, chased across
state line, life on the line—kicked down, kid-
napped, taken back. Some women breathe in
old dreams, slip under night cover, think
they stink on the sheets, knuckle under
enemy outposts in their minds.

Some women try to make it, fix it, get it
right, can't do anything right—beaten up,
beaten down, beaten to death between thin
walls, windows up. Some women start up
at the door slam, click of the briefcase clasp,
tinkle of ice in the glass, bourbon splashed
on the floor. Some women can't take any
more morning after sweet talk, panes out—
board it up, change the locks, bar the doors.

Some women—the ball-buster, castrators,
man-haters—stick out their tongues on a dare,
tear in the skin *(this is a pore war)*, go for
the muscle and scream: no more, bloody
spit ribboning lips, mouthy at the firing line
like they mean it. Some women take
a match to the gas, burn the bed, end up
rattling chains behind bars. Some women
want a revolution like a lover
and a full metal jacket for a heart.

Note: "this is a pore war" and "a revolution like a lover" are from Robin Morgan's *Monster*

Dina Ben-Lev

In Sweetness and in Light

Circling the lake path with Sarah turns serious.
Between us we've shredded thirteen men
during ten years of talking.
Breezes blow amber
leaves onto the water.
She says, He forgets
to have sex with me.

Ahead of us, a boy
smacks and smacks
his dripping dog
for diving into the ducks.
The retriever holds his stance,
nose to the ground.
I shake my head. Torch him, I say,

and she sighs. At our age we're used
to the spill between strange
and ordinary.... We pass a bench
where a white-haired woman in fatigues curses
a shopping cart; her sign reads, Donate
a New Dimension!

Sarah will likely leave this beau
and fall again. Chicory and almond rise
around us; when we go by, the coffee man
waves between machines, Hey gals,
want something wildly wet and molecular?
Out of earshot, she moans, Lord,
how a voice can ruin a landscape....

On the last stretch, we walk arm in arm,
faster, and in unison, like two avenging
Eves en route to tip the universe.
Tie him up, I hiss, and let him slide
down the driveway on his stomach. No,
she grins, I'll feed him and forgive him, then
I'll pull the pin.

Elisavietta Ritchie

Elegy for the Other Woman

May her plane explode
with just one fatality. But, should it not,
may the other woman spew
persistent dysentery from
your first night ever after.
May the other woman vomit
African bees and Argentine wasps.
May cobras uncoil from her loins.
May she be eaten not
by something dramatic like lions,
but by a wart-hog.
I do not wish the other woman
to fall down a well
for fear of spoiling the water,
nor die on the highway because
she might obstruct traffic.
Rather: something easy, and cheap,
like clap from some other bloke.
Should she nevertheless survive
all these critical possibilities,
may she quietly die of boredom with you.

Mary Kolada Scott

Brute Force

Your husband is brutal,
the trail guide told me
after she witnessed him
kick the horse with his heel
and yank the reins where
he wanted the mare to go.

He laughed when I told him later,
said he knew how to handle horses
and women. *They need a firm hand.*
You have to show them who's boss.

Years after I left his control,
I catch myself touching my throat
as if I still wear the imprints
of his fingers circling my neck
like a choker of pale amethysts.

I bridle at this intrusion of memory,
smarting as a swift kick to my ribs,
and gallop away, unharnessed.

Nancy Lynch Weiss

Listen for the Latchspring

Stomach's knotted up again
Shoulders seem so tense
Must be close to five o'clock
Doesn't make much sense

Listen for the latchspring
Hear the creaking door
Guess he's home for dinner
But it's only half past four

Hover near the oven
Or crouch beside the fridge
Depends what kind of day he's had
Or what mood he is in

Eager just to please him
Hungry for some love
Arms held wide to hug him
Are pushed off with a shove

Dinner isn't ready
Though she tries to explain why
Nothing ever pleases him
Except a fresh black eye

Children, children, don't come in
When he's beating me this way
Go and play a little while
'Til everything's okay

She huddles in the corner
Beside the kitchen door
Its promises of freedom
Sweep her off the floor

Listen for the latchspring
Hear the creaking door
Walk into the darkness
Won't pay that price no more

Dormant Strength

"Everything in me huddles where the wind leans,
holding out its scent like prayer."

—Susan Clayton-Goldner

Anne Wilson

Sunflower Forest

The year that I thought
nothing could grow
in my heart,
I planted hybrid sunflowers:
Vibrant yellows, aged bronze,
blood-red maroon,
sunbursts of tangerine,
all *alive* in thick forests of stalks
four and five feet tall.
And when they burst
like chariots of the sun
full-speed into bloom
above the deck,
I smiled
at their exuberant profusion,
knowing that
even in my year of desolation,
they would turn their
jewel-like leonine heads
to show me
the pathway of the sun
and point me lightward.

Marguerite McKirgan

Ghosts

Behind the door
Of a small dark room
In the basement of my old house
I found a boxful of sprouting potatoes
Forgotten in the spring planting

They had managed to grow
Without light
Without dirt
Their will to live
Superseding all obstacles

Their thin white sprouts
Reached up toward a fragile beam of light
Through a crack in the wall
In the late afternoon sun

I left them there
To see if these ghost sprouts
Might at least produce
The ghosts of potatoes

I was like that
Growing from my need to grow
Even in the dark
Growing when it was time
In spite of the darkness
And no dirt for my roots

Myrna Jackson

On Point

Out of a choked sky, gray
with marriage, I ditch
in a brown October pasture.
Empty. Wet. Cold.
Able to walk away whole,
I guzzle a chestful of air.

Like cows unmoved
by rain nuzzling the fall earth
for wisps of green,
I watched the traffic go by
every day. And I stayed.

But I was the one with the hands:
I strung the barbed wire,
dug the trenches,
and collected the clutter
from passing cars.

Now I explore vastness
in three empty rooms
and doubt I'll ever fill them
with more than a bed and chair.

Pavlova quivering on point,
Walenda tensed for his cue,
I stretch out the moment
in dizzy equipoise,
till gravity's dare.

P.M. Lovett

One Thursday

I woke up
drank tea
fed the boys
showered
dressed
went to school
taught, laughed
read and wrote
drove home
took them to swim lessons
watched them swim
helped with homework
ate dinner
sang songs
kissed them good night
cleaned the kitchen
did the laundry
checked the boys

sat down
lit a candle
smoked a cigarette
sipped some wine
listened to music
read a poem

and never once thought of you.

Leslie Lytle

How To Pray

Prayer is a single leaf in a cluttered
bouquet blooming into a tree
hundreds of years old. Concentrate on the veined
intricacies of the leaf. How the forked river
where tree blood flows could be the naked
tree branching, sketched in silhouette
posed against a green sky, if we push
resemblance too far we see ourselves—prayer

is like that: I pray for the man who hates me.
Concentrate on the leaf fringed with brown
disease fingering the edge as though someone touched
flame to the corner of a page and changed
her mind: she will not burn this letter. Why? Passion
lacking resolve disguises emotions we shun

owning. *Burn the leaf!* the enraged tree screams,
womanly, resentful of having my burdens
dumped on her metaphor. I move on to an especially
tall blade of grass in an unmowed yard. In a crowd,
whispers spoken behind my back are always his voice
talking about me. *Shut up and pray! Damn you,*
concentrate on the leaf! I try to imagine

the man who hates me saying. He likes to give
orders. Or is it advice? The tree is
sleeping now,
offers to pretend to be God if I promise
to speak in hushed tones and not wake her.

Susan Clayton-Goldner

The Space Between Colors

In another life, there may be dreams
to tell us why dirt roads
disappear into frames of paintings.
Our bodies won't matter,
will breeze open windows
like the smell of honeysuckle or rain,
not afraid of losing
what was never had
by having it.
What divides people steps outside itself
unable to remember the road
or the framework of trees surrounding it.

If I could lend autumn a face
to smile into the stillborn
space between colors,
maybe then I could forgive myself
for making the wrong choice;
whiten my lies and go on
into the dappled granite days
of what's missing.

But I cannot borrow from this dream.
The leaves that drift me to sleep
wait somewhere under a nightmare of stars
stone-heavy on my chest.
Everything in me huddles
where the wind leans
holding out its scent
like prayer.

Tammy Vitale

Things I Have Learned From My Garden

bumble bees sleep
beneath flower petals
antennae down, wings
tucked against their bodies

no matter what I put on top
to make things look good
if the soil is bad below
only weeds grow—some are pretty

bleeding hearts can't take
the heat around here
and grapes don't like
too much rain

snapdragons and gladiolus
with their glamorous blooms
will fall over
if not staked

the cat will eat the catnip
before it is ready
to be harvested
and enjoy it immensely

sometimes even when I do
everything
right, the tomatoes don't grow
and then sometimes they do

Lynn Asch

Survivor

This much I know for sure—
I am a survivor.
A year has passed since you left, and,
unable to eat or sleep, I nested in pillows
and rocked myself in mourning.
A year since I circled the kitchen,
freezing in coat and gloves
repeating and repeating
to drive the truth into my brain:
He's sleeping with another woman,
until that long night.
surrendered to dawn.

Then came the months of steel
when every thought of you
shot daggers into my heart.
With each word you spoke,
the blades entered my flesh deeper.
My knees buckled under their weight.
Couldn't you see the knife handles
sticking out of my sweater,
the blood running down my belly?
Life out there became fiction,
the inner world the only reality.

Now I trust the voice within
as she leads me through midnight caves
of pain and terror
to my self, my place of comfort.
Though I lose my footing
and slip down again into the blackness,
though your handwriting on an envelope
can impale me
in an instant, I know
I will continue
my journey home.

BARBARA HENDRYSON

Prayer for a Tenspeed Heart

Let the fire of my body
propel and warm me
and let each darkness
reveal its plenitude.

Let the hills flatten
under my wheels
and the eloquent curves
yield up their good surprise.

Let my heart be obstinate
when I need to climb
and my lowliest gears
restrain my spinning down.

Let there be flatland, too,
and into that glittering place
let me stretch with the heart of a lover:
at full speed, blind, and intent.

Supporting Roles

"...tinged with a shade of faint regret the once-loved always wear."

—Frances Witte

Elisabeth Murawski

The Audience

The divorce is young, has barely cut
its first tooth. He stands beside her bed,
cap in hand, supplicant, uneasy satellite
circling the wrong planet.

"Then die!" he had told her once, angry with her
off the wagon. Now she's doing it,
a yellow-skinned stick figure
burning up the sheets.

Where is the beauty he married? Above
soft aquarium noises—oxygen
bubbling though tubing—he whispers:
"I love you." The strawberry hairs

on his wrist gleam as he pours it
in her ear like a poison. Hearing,
she jerks her head. Her mouth
gropes for a no. Too weak for lies

she signals "go" with a flutter
of long bony fingers. Perplexed,
defeated, he exits, she dies. Later,
he will tell his story with a tease

of bewilderment, clutching a cache
of good intentions to his breast,
letting it spill down the front
of his shirt like a cheap, garish tie.

Patti Tana

The Words

And at the end   the words
held us together

talking through the night
the dear sounds
carried us across the country
across the years
to our joining

our words appeared like stars
spelling the names
we named ourselves.

On the eve of our divorce
I sat alone in a dark concert hall
listening to poets
trying to stop the end
of the world with words.

All I could think of was the night
before we gave birth
holding hands in a concert hall
water dripping onto the floor.

After his birth
and after you went home exhausted
from helping my body   let go
of our gift
I lay still in a dark room
my hand gripping the phone
your voice pouring happy happy
into my ears for years

for years
the sound of your voice
lit the room
and hummed in my body.

At the break
I hurried from the poets' hall
hurried to the train
water dripping on my face
hurried home to our last night.

And at the end   the words
loosened my grip on your hand
and helped me let go.

Janie Breggin

Prison Camp

I was enchanted
            bewitched
            besotted
            baited
            trapped
            hooked
run to ground
run aground
ground down.

I climbed over glass teeth
where broken bottle shards guard the wall
scrabbled down ladderless brick
with scraped raw elbows and knees
crawled under the razor wire
                                        sprockets
                                        fish hooks and
                                        wood screws
                                        iron brambles
                                        dipped in blood
                                        gone to rust.

Here,
where wire is barbed
            barbarous
            bearded
            blood-blackened,

these

    (not the wedding ring
    so easily removed,
    but so long remembered)

these

    are the binds that tie.

Francine Witte

Mother-in-Law

We never met. I knew you only
from his voice hunching up
with your name. His first loss.
Each autumn, on the anniversary,
he'd light a thick candle, let it burn
into another year you wouldn't have.
I once saw him sob for a woman
on TV whose cancer, like yours, wouldn't heal.
When we visited the school where you taught,
I watched as he stood and stood by a tree
with your name. By now, you know

he's remarried. Children and all.
On nights like this, just past summer,
air crisp as apple-skin, you and I
almost meet. There we are in a swirl
of thought just above his head.
You with your dress the color of wrong
sunlight that funerals sometimes have, and me
tinged with a shade of faint regret
the once-loved always wear.
The two of us transparent, real
as breath, our hands about to touch.

J.B. Bernstein

Tanglewood

in memory of Marshall, my ex-husband

I was walking to the Shed, a musical oasis warming up
when I came upon an ugly duckling of a tree: disabled,
disadvantaged, isolated by an act of God or some such thing.
It fascinated me: the form snubbed its nose at Mother Nature.
I stumbled over swollen roots, was pricked by an outspoken
branch as I circled to the front. At least, I thought it was
the front. The trunk was uneven, lopsided. Its crunchy bark
snarled in self-defense, piny arms groping for attention.

I had left you at the Inn in a straight-back chair, sitting
like it would electrocute at any moment. When I returned,
you were staring at the side of the TV set, punishing yourself
for not coming—as if cancer weren't a reason
good enough. Later, as if still married, we traipsed to the lobby
where you found a red velvet couch so stiff it made you
sit erect. I chose a rocking chair with soft, plush, purple
cushions. We ordered Baileys on the rocks: the coffee-colored
creme ripened memory and soon we laughed so hard and long,
our bodies swooned like dissipated lovers.

SANDRA GARDNER

Love Story

when she finally
after 15 years said
I've had enough
I'm calling a lawyer
he said
go ahead
you'll starve to death
you won't get a job and
        no one will want you at 45
I'm taking the car   *house*   *and kids*
but don't forget   he said   *I love you*

when her lawyer
got a court date
he said
go ahead
my lawyer will screw your lawyer,
it'll be a piece of cake
but don't forget   he said   *I love you*

they had their day
in the courthouse coffeeshop
where the lawyers   hers and his
talked golf and fees while their clients
had coffee and cake that stuck in their throats
along with the settlement
that wasn't settled
at separate tables

when they were finally
decreed legally asunder
after every shred of their married life
had been paragraphed and claused,
she left the house
turning away from the children
she saw his face
mirrored in the window
mouthing the words
                    don't forget

Rose Mary Sullivan

Goodbye and Goodbye

The deceased specified
that his ashes be
scattered in the garden
among his vegetables
and flowers.

Does his widow carefully
rinse each petal
of every sweet petunia
each leaf of lettuce
every onion and tomato
carried into their house?

Does she wash some remains
down the drain
and unknowingly swallow
unseen particles
of the recently departed
with her salad?

An unsavory process
my ex-husband's ashes
recycled in this manner
by his third wife.

Even after many years
I still wished him
a more gentle departure.

The Patterns Continue

*"Curled once again like a fetus not yet launched,
she descends toward the monotonous
duplications of history."*

—Adrian Blevins

LAVONNE J. ADAMS

The Math of Marriage

My mother's marriages were intricate equations:
a carmine eye equals chocolate nestled
in crimped paper encompassed by
elegant embossed cardboard; a house,
a car, and a pantry boxed like a city
skyline are greater than or equal to
the square root of separate bedrooms.

By example, I learned advanced math
of marriage—how to divide
pie charts of time, to graph
the intersection of wants—*y*, his;
x, mine. Among infinite variables,
I could not attain my marital
equation's missing variable:

Y + Home + Children = Happiness.
Ultimately, I understood
theorems: the division of divorce—
bank accounts halved and beds vacated—
does not equal exponential unhappiness.
Consider the alternative:
living in a null set.

Adrian Blevins

The Wilderness You Know Best

All the notable things that ever happened to you
happened out of love. Your mother, Titan blonde and thin
and a woman with so many words in her mouth it's a wonder
they didn't just fall out of her in a twelve-point font
while she stood at the stove over sweet-and-sour chicken,
left you one night. The shadow in her wake was so immense,
such a fucking prelude, it fell all the way into the nineties
like a fashion you saw coming, but couldn't predict.
She'd fallen in love, that's the thing, with a man
who made objects out of wood. But all the time before that
your father had been slinking out of bed to meet some student
or another at the motel down the road, so you can't blame her.
You'd like to talk to those girls now, to ask them what they thought
they were doing with your father. You'd like to buy them a drink,
invite them into your house to look each of your sons in the eye
and then you'd serve them—you'd serve them champagne
and a very chocolate cake. Listen, it was the early seventies
and you don't blame anyone for having a heart. If you'd been
your mother, you would have fallen in love with the wooden
man. You would have gone anywhere with him, ridden a horse
to the holy land, tied your own hands up with the great generosity
of unsullied lust. And if you'd been one of your father's students,
you would have wanted him out of his house, and you
would not have considered his wife there, or his daughters,
or anything at all but that he might love you enough to die for.
And that is what it always comes to, no matter the decade, no matter

whose body: wanting to be buried alive in solace, shoved feeble
into time undying with what you didn't get when you needed it most,
with what wasn't there when you were eleven and sat in flannel
on the staircase while X drooled after Y and Y fell from Z. You were there,
you saw it, and the scent of sex screaming to be let out, and the odors
of bourbon and vodka and the high-blown sounds of someone on a trumpet
and grass smoke and—what could you have done but put your hands
under your chin and survey from above all the pretty heads lower
down? And whatever the adults were saying, it's clear most of that
was lies, or immaterial—Nixon was out, okay, and hurrah, but that's not
what's most in you now, not the part that was sucked up
as through a straw into the future. No, Sugar: you were born
to go on tapping at your chest as the seasons sing their demands
inside you, born to go on living, to cut a path through a trail of heartbreak
toward the auspicious wilderness you know best, to traverse backward
toward the dwelling of all initiation, to tread crazy into the inflated heart
of the one who will not betray you, into the riveted body of the only one
who will not let you go.

ANDRENA ZAWINSKI

Unexcused Absences for 3 Men + 1 Experiment in the Genetics of Heart

1. Heart failure. (Father, long gone.)

I've never forgiven you for dying, for the way
you turned my mother under the weight of you
bare-boned and alone outside the confederacy
of couples. She, one instead of two, volunteered
in America in the sixties to go under the knife
for a clitoridectomy, to vow her fidelity to a bottle
of sodium-butysol to keep the feelings at bay
in the shadow of the other
with a new addiction
to howling.

2. Heart attack. (Ex-husband.)

I'll never forgive you for walking out the way
it was then in the heat of a summer first love,
kundalini love, for flying off into the western sky
as I, outside the expectancy of couples breathing in
their easy deliveries, hummed *nam myo ko renge kyo*
to make my way down the charity ward to go for
an episiotomy, long labor, hard birth
where I would not flinch
but found my pitch
in screaming.

3. Arteries Hardening. (Son, moved away.)

I could have forgiven you for finding your way
away, but not for your abandon of these things
I have been saving for years, the hand-sewn swan
hung at the crib, pocket stuffed with rattles and toys,
go-to-sleep books, music box charm too fancy for a boy.
You romance the keys now, strung out on the chain
of hearts outside the intimacy of coupling,
sworn to your own singular
winged promises
but singing.

4. Heart on the Line. (Love, lost causes.)

I can never forgive myself for wanting any one
of you here beside me now to lighten up this long
night riddling the dark with reason and rhyme,
pretending some glade would open wide inside
skirts of morning fog, that I could take on my own
wings, scale the fantailed clouds, hold close
to the heart a light bauble of moon, wake
with you from a sleep
cell, double-helixed
and only dreaming.

MELISSA PRUNTY KEMP

Liberation

1

You were married with two kids,
a husband with a corporate job,
a house and a Mercedes,
the bridge club and the Junior League.
You grew up white/wonderbread;
nothing more American than that.

Then one day came
the knock/you/down truth.
You're white/wonderbread
the maid/mother/lover
a cardigan shell,
straight brown hair
(neatly French-braided).
Your husband leaves you
for baby/blonde hair
baby/blue orbs
sixteenth-year old curves,
a tan and no wrinkles,
ready all the time.

And where does this leave you?
Divorced and wanting sex
and a job
(other than cleaning baby shit)
and an identity
not linked to a man.

2

"Welcome home, sister,"
say the uptown dykes.
And you say, "why not,"
but I've got to find a nice woman
not one of those   sign-carrying, frayed-white-used-to-be-blue-
jean-wearing, sporting bald haircuts and nit-nipple-displaying
Amazons,

but one who has a stylish cut
                    (not too short)
    wears Calvin Klein and Versace
drives the right car
                    (a BMW will do).

And after ten years,
On the last bar of
"Start all Over"
came the TRUTH:
You're white/wonderbread,
a lover/sucker,
equality-maid,
pseudo-lesbian/mother,
still cleaning up shit.

Your lover leaves you
for baby dykes, virgin cunts
still smelling of adolescence,
ready double/time.

And where does it leave you?
Wanting sex
        and an identity
        not linked to a man.

Diane Lutovich

0 Into 0

It was good she was good
at long division,
dividing endlessly since 4th grade—
major division at first marriage—
one heart fragmented
two worthless halves, then the child took half
of each half worth anything,
suddenly   not even a remainder

When the first marriage collapsed, place settings
by two, paintings by 4 (she got 1/4)
child by thirds (she got 2/3 time). Instead
of dividing ancient Indian spears by two,
he kept
both. Same with money—
a lot of division reduced
nothing to nothing.

Then the series of men;
dividing five into one, not easy
unless willing to deal
with decimals or points—
not much left over,
remainders like dividends,
too small

Now comes the second prime factor man
whole number craving division—nights or days
2 into 7 leaving him
alone three nights. Dividing
without multiplying,
share the remainder—or maybe the remainder
is really
the divisor or possibly, the dividend.

Meanwhile, the daughter of the 2nd marriage,
without dividing loyalty, grows up, starts dividing
hope by fear. Learning to separate
dividend from quotient from divider.

What's left? Still dividing the body from soul
finally, earth from promise.

Adrian Blevins

The Inheritance

She walks tiptoe though shattered glass,
across thrown-out goblets and crystal
punch bowls, so who couldn't have guessed
she would one day falter, then,
like a slow motion star, fall? For years
it's been happening, this dull death
of her married heart. But because
he won't hear her say it, puts a flat hand
over her mouth and a *just listen* into the air,
she dreams of the night twenty years ago
her mother, furious, fled into the light
of something better. That's when her father told her,
wrapped in invisible bandages, that it was over.
He said it was the diminished all abated,
a minus sign, a perpetual winter, and an empty bucket
in a dried-up river in an old burned book.
So thinking now of the other life
she might have had if she'd heard him in that darkness,
thinking of the ways she might tell her husband
she must fail him now as they failed her,
remembering how her father wept even years later
in the kitchen, how he looked into her face
and told her she was more like him
than like the bitch who had left them both,
she enters, marked like a sinking vessel, into the body
of her young mother. There in that nest,
curled once again like a fetus not yet launched,
she descends toward the monotonous duplications
of history. So who will blame her
such long losses? And what will rise to lift her from them
now that they are named?

The Past in Present Light

"No doubt about it—he has grown smaller…"

—Arlene L. Mandell

Dina Ben-Lev

Driving

1

The summer our marriage failed
we picked sage to sweeten our hot dark car.

We sat in the yard with heavy glasses of iced tea,
talking about which seeds to sow

when the soil was cool. Praising our large, smooth
spinach leaves, free this year of Fusarium wilt,

downy mildew, blue mold. And then we spoke of flowers,
and there was a joke, you said, about old florists

forced to make other arrangements.
Delphiniums flared along the back fence.

All summer it hurt to look at you.

2

I heard a woman on the bus say, "He and I were going
in different directions." As if it had something to do

with latitudes or tides. Trying to write down
how love empties itself from a house, how a view

changes, how the sign for infinity turns into a noose
for a couple. Trying to say that weather weighed

down all the streets we traveled on, that if gravel sinks,
it keeps sinking. How can I blame you who kneeled day

after day in wet soil, pulling slugs from the seedlings?
You who built a ten-foot arch for the beans, who hated

a bird feeder left unfilled. You who gave
carrots to a gang of girls on bicycles.

3

On our last trip we drove through rain
to a town lit with vacancies.

We'd come to watch whales. At the dock we met
five other couples—all of us fluorescent,

waterproof, ready for the pitch and frequency
of the motor that would lure these great mammals

near. The boat chugged forward—trailing a long,
creamy wake. The captain spoke from a loudspeaker:

In winter, gray whales love Laguna Guerrero; it's warm
and calm, no killer whales gulp down their calves.

Today we'll see them on their way to Alaska. If we
get close enough, observe their eyes—they're bigger

than baseballs, but can only look down. Whales can
communicate at a distance of 300 miles—but it's

my guess they're all saying, *Can you hear me?*
His laughter crackled. When he told us Pink Floyd is slang

for a whale's two-foot penis, I stopped listening.
The boat rocked, and for two hours our eyes

were lost in the waves—but no whales surfaced, blowing
or breaching or expelling water through baleen plates.

Again and again you patiently wiped the spray
from your glasses. We smiled to each other, good

troopers used to disappointment. On the way back
you pointed at cormorants riding the waves—

you knew them by name: the Brants, the Pelagic,
the double-crested. I only said, I'm sure

whales were swimming under us by the dozens.

4

Trying to write that I love the work of an argument,
the exhaustion of forgiving, the next morning,

washing our handprints off the wineglasses. How I loved
sitting with our friends under the plum trees,

in the white wire chairs, at the glass table. How you
stood by the grill, delicately broiling the fish. How

the dill grew tall by the window. Trying to explain
how camellias spoil and bloom at the same time,

how their perfume makes lovers ache. Trying
to describe the ways sex darkens

and dies, how two bodies can lie
together, entwined, out of habit.

Finding themselves later, tired, by a fire,
on an old couch that no longer reassures.

The night we eloped we drove to the rain forest
and found ourselves in fog so thick

our lights were useless. There's no choice,
you said, we must have faith in our blindness.

How I believed you. Trying to imagine
the road beneath us, we inched forward,

gently honking, again and again.

Magi Stone

The Past in Present Light

You never understood how metaphors nourished me,
more than twenty year-old scotch,
expensive foreign cars,
or your standards of fine living.

Pink ideas take wing in my head,
like a flock of flamingoes.
They nest in my imagination,
feather mature, fly onto the paper.

You never got the hang of imagination.
After all, it can't be measured with a slide rule,
drawn with a T-square,
or plotted on a circuit board,

Like the blueprints for the house
you designed without a site in mind,
I was forced to roll you up tightly,
store you away with other failed dreams.

Your energy is still Ivy League; harnessed
in your original college class jacket.
You are a strict practitioner of hard core,
button-down, wing-tipped success.

Years ago my walls were hung
with tears and wailing. Now,
poetry pushes me up and around the room,
filling it with satisfaction. Life glows with
the light that comes from make-believe.

After we were exiled from the Garden of Eden,
we replanted the convictions we carried away.
You grow a forest of Sequoias. Beneath a lilac bush,
I nurture white violet words, wild and fragrant.

Linda Goodman Robiner

Where She Lives

She moved from her father's house
to her husband's without ever a place
that was hers, didn't appear in the streets

of the city without a man 'til she was
nearly fifty. Books belonged to her, blouses
in the closet, but the house was not hers.

The man didn't know her name. Her
inner life was scrawled on scraps of paper
stashed under a pile of bras, lacy

in her drawer. Years later, she read stories
about archeologists, excavated the notes
and questions she'd buried in earlier times.

Rebecca McClanahan

First Husband

After the marriage exploded, it sifted
down to this: the scar your fist left
on the filing cabinet where I kept my poems,
and on the ironing board stacks of Army khakis
whose pleats never flattened to your satisfaction.
It helped to think of you that way, a detonation
searing my eyes from everything but the white flash
that lit my path years later to a place
where I was still young enough to pass
as a bride. I've kept you hidden, even my friends
don't know. And I had almost buried you
when the Christmas card came—your fourth wedding,
complete with children acquired along the way.
Your chest has dropped, and gone completely
is the hairline that began its early retreat
when you were still the boy I would marry.
Your shirt is wrinkled; beside you
the new wife is already starting to fade.
Something in her chin reminds me of me. I send
my best wishes. For finally after twenty years
a memory ripens and falls into my lap:
our last trip, a Canadian forest
where strange animals destined for extinction
roamed the green hills. At a roadside stand
we stopped for melons. Later you steered
with one hand, and all the way down the mountain
I licked the sweetness from your fingers.

Frances Isaacs Gilmore

Provincetown Hook

That old Commercial Street garage
where you bought a pulley makes me sad;
paint too fresh, too vermilion;
I took it for a firehouse. They sell
high achiever shoes now, Birkenstocks
and platforms with deeply notched tread.

The pulley had a heavy iron hook;
oval, but the inside was angular,
straight lines and corners. I loved you
for picking out the satisfying weighty form
with your filmmaker's unfailing eye.

Why should I be sad?
That was nearly thirty years ago;
I am better married now.
Wouldn't I be sadder if the old shop
were still there, full of relics
of seafaring life: lanterns
with charred wicks and chipped paint,
smooth iron eyes for rope two inches thick,
foghorns, brass compasses and ships'
wheels with the varnish worn?
No, I would still treasure the old shop's nostalgia
as I struggled past my own.

I feel a different, sweeter sadness
at the Truro dunes—or is it joy?
like encountering a long lost lover;
but these are not the twisting corridors
of love for a man and loss;
more like an endless, sunlit room
where I have always lived in secret:
sand, little grass fountains,
chipped bowl hills painted
with a palette of soft greens and always
the promise of the sea beyond
the last ridge.

Barbara DeCesare

A Truth Like Blood

There is dishonesty
in a neat wound. One that bleeds
just enough.

I have heard of the man
bravely staggering into an emergency room with
an arrow through the eye,
a bullet in the breast.

He will live.

If it had been one inch,
one millimeter,
one acre,
one mile,
one thousand years to the left
he would have died.

He would have at least bled and bled.

Instead he has a tiny scar,
perfect vision,
no slurred speech, and years later,
when the new wife undresses him
it will be so insignificant
that she will not ask.

Dodie Messer Meeks

Not To Be Embarrassing About It

We thought we had
well, we called it
a marriage
all those years
then one morning he was shaving
and I was yanking on my pantyhose
swearing at a run
and one of us said
the ultimate wrong word.
The whole thing came undone
like a dogfood bag
when you finally find the red thread.

Now when we run into each other
we smile the smile you smile
if you bump into a store mirror
or a mannequin
and come up with an apologetic grin
before you snap
that it's actually nobody.

Stellasue Lee

Report

I read it in the newspaper,
a woman, naked,
covered in blood,
was seen walking
the old Townsgate section
of Westlake.
The police were called,
but when they arrived
she had disappeared.

I tell you this now: It was me;
stripped, bare, bloodied,
I walked from my marriage.
That was last winter.
My footprints were quickly shrouded
with brightly covered leaves
of orange and gold.
This is California after all;
a sun without ending
devours the years.

Arlene L. Mandell

The Ex

No doubt about it
he has grown smaller
his dark curls no more
than a few greasy wires
pressed across his scalp

but that voice is the same—
deep, genial—a voice
that could sell snake oil
to a snake.

Dodie Messer Meeks

Advice to a Bride

Dear little ladies with sweet little voices
have ended upended on ant teeming slopes
or after a tiff have been dropped from a cliff
or turned in the wind on slow turning ropes

Girls who have had the last word every argument
have eaten those words in a cold dungeon keep
or languished in stocks or been fed glowing rocks
or listened to Leno and given up sleep.

Ladies with tongues far less acid than mine can be
gurgled on guillotine, writhed on the rack.
All that I have to fear—tell me I'm lucky, dear—
is the dark certainty: he won't be back.

All my proud sisterhood, swearing you will be good,
wishing the hell you could leave it unsaid:
bare your arm. Make a fist. Tattoo it on your wrist.
Never correct a man's grammar in bed.

KATHI HENNESSY

Se*man*tics

Virtue, so they say,
comes from the Latin
virtus for manliness
and worth, to mean
chastity, *especially*
in a woman.

Under *irony*, they
do not say, *see*
virtue.

Leslie Lytle

The Blue Barrel

I need to describe the swimming-pool-blue barrel
posed against the naked bones of winter.
The walking stick trees in my wood lot
understand feeling purged of meaning,
January, being leafless. My estranged husband
left the barrel behind, fifty-five gallon
capacity for storing agricultural
chemicals—a concept I understand
objectively ("weed control"), subjectively
a mystery like my college days fling
with LSD (What did inducing
insanity have to do with expanding
my consciousness? What does poison have to do
with growing things?). Of blue fiberglass
construction, cracked, fouled with hazardous
compounds, the barrel cannot be discarded
at the dump, besides my husband would object
(*I might need it*, he would say.
For what? I would not ask. I failed to grasp the primary
function, the barrel's secondary function looms
surreal as cloud spit to my mind). I try
to imagine our lovemaking, fill
the void with sweaty bodies sans faces
borrowed from "R" rated films: we screwed,
spawned two sons. There must have been, though, a morning
cup of coffee we shared, some moment where passion
infused the act—take the blue plastic barrel,
(Take it? I wish someone would. *Please, take it*.)
bright with meaning in spite of the gray grass.

Mary E. O'Dell

Once Again I Dream About the Ex-Husband

A Charlie Chaplin toy man
complete with derby
and shapeless black suit

hangs himself
from my dining room chandelier
by his own necktie.

Reluctant to merely cut him down
and ruin the tie
I watch my fingers fumble with the knot.

After all, he isn't dead.
His eyelids flutter and there is that weak
apologetic grin.

Arlene L. Mandell

Bridal Veil

Reflected in a gilded mirror, the bride
leans forward, her breath a moist oval
on the glass. Her fingers tug
at the veil that won't fall
in graceful folds.

Wet your lips, the photographer orders
and she obeys, arranges her mouth
in a smile, but when the portrait
is delivered, her golden eyes
are like gray stones.

Two decades later she finds the photo
buried under old sweaters, examines
the sweet face, wets her lips
and smiles into the camera,

the veil lifted, at last,
from her life.

Beginning Again

*"Let your new self emerge, let it swing up into the sky,
let it fling into space and outward, discovering
world upon world upon world."*

—Joanne McCarthy

Patti Tana

The Last Tear

I shall wear black
    my feet slippered in slow step
        my arms waving lonely! lonely!

I shall drape sad mirrors with white sheets
    sit on a crate made of wood
        smear my body with ashes.

I shall rip my clothes and rise naked
    drench my skin in the sea
        flush my pores clean of his scent.

And when I cry the last tear I will catch it
    and place it high in my east window
        so every dawn will splash the day!

Barbara Hendryson

Hearts Are Like That

Don't underestimate a heart. Don't
call it "dear" as if it were
something to be condescended to.

And don't speak
of a "broken heart." It's stronger
than both of us put together.

Imagine its red glow; feel
how it beats for you tirelessly,
how it keeps perfect time.

Then think of the way it nourishes
all of your working parts,
the inlets and outlets that are you.

Think of your heart as a ball
made of rubber bands; feel how firm
and malleable it is in your hands;

then throw it against something
hard as you can. Do you see
how it comes right back to you

with no cracks or damages,
no little smithereens?
Notice, in the careless hands

of a child or thoughtless lover,
its resiliency. It's not a glass
bauble, or a valentine. It's a muscle

like a big truck or a boxing glove.
It saves you again and again.

Nancy Means Wright

Acrophobia

Fay's reading Virginia Woolf: how
a woman ought to have five hundred
pounds and a room of her own. Fay's got
the room all right—six flights up and over-

looking Video King; if you lean out
the bathroom window you see a slice
of sky and sometimes the handle
on the Dipper. But Fay's got acrophobia.

Open the window: her knees quake,
belly wheezes, blood leaks into her knuckles
and Fay collapses in a bang of bones.
Still Woolf holds something for Fay:

how many older women walk out with only
a sack on the back, rocks in the pocket—
where's the five hundred pounds now?
So Fay sticks stars on the bathroom ceiling,

half moon over the toilet, To The Light-
house next to the Zinfandel by the four-legged
tub; red Gloxinia in the window and snap-
shots of the grand-kids in each cracked

pane. When Fay gets a yen for the Dipper
she looks at those faces: one has the grin
Fay had in school the time she told them
Uncle Frank was F.D.R. in the White House:

for a whole week until they found out
Fay was the big kid in town, Fay was
a star on the ceiling, her own Big
Dipper. Fay was a Room of her Own.

Dina Ben-Lev

Home on New Year's

Never mind about being alone. At least
when you need it, the bathroom's
unoccupied. Couples won't wander into
your closets. And you can drink champagne
casually, contemplatively, in the way of the old rich.
Click on the TV and everyone'll be talking
too loud, blitzed on beer, or nervous
in sequins. Suddenly, an aerial view of Manhattan:
streets zig-zagging with lights, like a puzzle
burning apart at its seams. If it will,
let the planet crack into pieces, you're not
waiting for a countdown. Go ahead, throw confetti
on the rug. Pour your glass again, and if
the phone rings, don't answer, think,
Somebody always wants me.

Joanne McCarthy

The Vagina Poem

for Cathy Song

No, my vagina doesn't want to talk.
It has nothing to say.
It is tired from years of giving birth
to one big-headed child after another,
stretching not enough at first
and then too much. It wants
to put its feet up and
take life easy.

Yes, it hated the probing speculum
and it still does.
It didn't like tampons, the necessary mess,
and it probably liked men too much.
But recently it has retired.
It will write you a poem some day.
Right now it studies the Inner Self
and plans a trip to Tortuga.
It's happy.
Leave it alone.

Tania Rochelle

Feeding the Worms

for Greg

You think this is going to be a poem about death,
but it's really about being hungry all the time.
It's about craving sweets, even though I don't eat sugar
because of my past history of killing off
pound-bags of candy corn and wedding cookies
so I could puke them up like childhood shame
before my daily descent into a bottle.
It's about having kids when I knew better—three,
with a man who vanished into his creole spices,
polished silver, jazz ringing the glassware,
and the slick smiles of young women ready to serve.
It's about a chafing cat-lick of a marriage
that eventually rubbed me raw, and the divorce,
a bad disease that started as a rash,
and later, a man who kisses me like I'm clean,
like there is nowhere else he wants to go.
It's about telling this man he needs to take Vermox
because at least one of my kids has pinworms,
and how, these days, I hang my head in the toilet
searching shit for signs of parasites
as if they were the threads of my life unraveling
and I could stitch them back together again.

The whole family has to be treated, and I can't
figure out a way to tell him this
without implying he's part of the family.
And that might scare him away, the very thought
of being part of a family with worms,
with an eight-year-old who plays Boxcar Children
barefoot in the dirt, baking cakes
of grass and sticks, who pretends her father's dead,
that she could bear to lose her mother too.
Or part of a woman who's spent so much of her life
in the bathroom, on her knees. See,
this is not a poem about death, not yet,
but a love poem, my first.

Magi Stone

Renaissance Summer

Skidding into delayed adolescence,
my man, high in his heat, searches
for greener ferns to sear.

Unbraided end of myself hangs limp.
What is left for me? Days so long
the hours push, lengthening them.
I reconsider old values, passing years.

The convergence of the Medieval
prospective point is a lie!
There is no horizon.
It is easy to get lost.

Life's chosen road narrows,
crumbles at the edges, STOPS.
Sun and clouds divide the sky into equal pieces.
An unfinished woman, I reconstruct myself.
Search for a new fate.

The woman of the bones casts yarrow sticks.
Amber shafts of future darken the ground.
Armed with hours of prayer, wind spirits
chant answers low and gray.

My new life is established on quilt-comfort
melodies of Mother Goose rhymes;
reminding me that no one owns pain and grief forever.

Clay remembers the hands that made it.
Beauty locked bone deep emerges remodeled.
I ensilk my legs in green stockings like stems;
make my hair the color of apricots.
Now I am ripe enough to begin again.

June Owens

Luminous Lady

The final papers came today.
So I say to myself:
Hey, Luminous Lady, heavy girl,
If you want a new deep love,
Be grateful you are you.
Some boys, sweetie, admire
A big woman whose thighs
Rub one another when she walks,
Whose buttocks roll
Against the fabric
of her flower dress;
A woman, like you, who has arms
That are really arms,
Venus arms to cover and hold.
Some men, remember,
Love to be smothered
In sweet-smelling flesh—
Back to the bosom
Back to the womb—
That's a man's innermost,
And secret desire.
So I say to myself:
Be grateful for your genes.
What did your ex know?
You are the answer
To a special man's dreams.

LAUREL SPEER

Candyman

I meet my first husband in the desert. This isn't
the beautiful, complicated desert of animals, plants,
hillocks and varieties of green. This is the flat,
desolate stretch off I-10. He gestures for me to get
in the car. He's imperious, elegant, well-dressed.
His hair is styled and he's finally found out
what to do about those hangnails.

I have a little water left in my canteen. It's warm
and metallic. The canteen inside its holder bangs
against my hip and dangles at an awkward angle
from the metal eyelets of the web belt on which
it's hooked. Very boss, very rakish, death-defying
and childish. But I do not get into that car.

Lynn Asch

Footsteps

Footsteps following an ancient path
leaving behind the familiar, the everyday,
the certain. Footsteps making fresh tracks
in the snow, moving through blue space
uncovering the mystery. Footsteps
leading in new directions, striking out
on their own, being bold.

I think of footsteps now, remembering you
and how we were together. How laughter
was our medicine, and love our daily meal.
I think of you and our footsteps
intertwining, weaving a tapestry
of love and family and home.
I think of you and our footsteps drifting,
taking different paths, tearing us apart.
I think of you and feel the tears we shed
in the silence of our hearts.
I think of you and remember the rending
of the fabric we had made.
How I feel today the frayed threads still
woven through me, the ends without
connections that always used to be.

I think of you and all our footsteps,
the ones that set me dancing
and those that sent me searching
toward a separate goal—the coming
to awareness in new, expanded places.
I look back at all those footsteps
and how they brought me here
to the tops of distant mountains,
to inner worlds I'd never known,
to fulfillment of dreams
I'd never dared dream.

I am thankful for our footsteps
for the dancing and the pain.
I am grateful for the journey
and the gifts along the way.

Janet I. Buck

Popped Umbrellas

Since my first marriage
had the flavor of old bubble gum.
Since my second was musical
chairs of a prison camp.
The only treeline being that
of need and deep sea dire
depressing tides where smiles
broke rules and were not tolerated,
where temples of tempers
stole cushions from hearts
and sex went solo, sadly enough.

I had a number of serious
sentence fragments
when it came to willing.
Of course, when love drifts by,
you jump on without much choice,
like a moving sidewalk
that jets toward joy
you just can't stop.
Dread's designated driver
gets drunk and you don't mind much.
Old brown boxes of sour fairy tales
are overdue library books
in the back seat of an old sedan,
so you return them shyly
and proceed as hummingbirds
that respect the flutter
of passion's heated wings.

Love's hieroglyphics
are kin to honeydew:
you just sense when
the season is right and slit it
when the moment strikes.
And we did.
Touchdowns came so naturally.
Umbrellas popping to meet clean rain.

Stellasue Lee

My Name Is Stellasue

Which means star and violet
as though a deep purple of longing
is the narrow band of light
that spreads unto it's own spectrum.
Blue-white I burn

for the cool touch of a man
to still the vagrant ghost
of loneliness at midnight.
Hear the wind?
Quickly, quickly it gathers

kindness spilled in sleep
no other world can offer.
I sparkle with heaven's grace,
feel the weight of winter's approach,
the silence and gentle gloom of years.

Deep in the blue well of my eyes
lives a raggedy child-spirit
whose voice awakens as a variable star;
bone by bone, breath by breath,
named perfect

in my imperfections,
transcendent of plain face,
breasts, sloping shoulders—
ablaze with consuming desire.

Joan Jobe Smith

Picking the Lock on the Door to Paradise

You probably won't believe this
but I am in San Francisco on the
corner of Lombard and Van Ness
on the seventh floor of a hotel
overlooking the Golden Gate
Bridge and I am drinking Dom
Perignon champagne and teaching a
tall dark and handsome poet
to dance the fox trot to Frank
Sinatra's "Our Love is Here to
Stay" and he won't do a thing I say,
won't let me lead, won't agree
I'm a better dancer because
I was a go-go dancer for seven
years. He says he could dance
the fox trot if he wanted to,
after all he can bugaloo to
The Doors's "L.A. Woman" but
he doesn't want to dance the
fox trot and when I laugh, he
does too and sits down next to
the window, sips beer and peers
out at the Golden Gate Bridge
and I don't give a damn if he
ever learns to dance the fox
trot, the waltz, cha-cha, or
the Charleston, because he is
a tall dark and handsome poet
and we are in San Francisco
peering out at the Golden Gate
Bridge that is disappearing
into a sunset fog, and our
love is here to stay.

JOANNE MCCARTHY

Sea Change

I want to be buried with my wedding ring—
you said it so many times.
Like your grandmother stiff in her coffin
wearing her wide cold band,
you wanted to die clearly labeled *Beloved Wife*.
You could never remove that slim circle.
Taped to your finger, it trundled
through delivery of each new child;
it became what you were: mother, wife.

Whatever pulled him away, whatever shape
his changed love finally took is not important.
You did not die. Surprised beyond belief
at what you could endure, your heart kept beating,
lungs pumped and bowels emptied.
The meaningless ring you tore from your finger in tears.
Later you carried it carefully in your pocket
to a point overlooking the water.
You hurled it high and far out
over the tops of madronas
watching it glitter and turn,
arc into fall, dropping swiftly
to beach and water below.

Let the gold ring encrust and turn green.
Let it lie in the maw of the great octopus
that lurks beneath the blue Sound.
Let your old love plunge under that surface,
let that old self slip into the water,
a corpse no diver will find.
Let your old self be buried with your wedding ring
fulfilling your vow, and who you are now
is another, no wife but a woman.
Let your new self emerge, let it swing up into the sky,
let it fling into space and outward, discovering
world upon world upon world.
Never look backward or down.
Your new life is waiting, you feel it.
Very well, then: learn to begin.

Karen Ethelsdattar

The First Time I Married

The first time I married
I took my husband's name for mine
and added Mrs.
I pulled it over my ears, a woolen cap,
even when it scratched in warm weather.
I was his falcon, hooded.
I was his pigeon, banded.
I sank into his name like a feather bed
and neglected to rise in the morning.
I crept under his wing
like a fledgling
too small to spread its own feathers.

Now I add your name to mine,
proud and frightened.
This time I keep my own,
I surrender nothing.
Still this act
reminds me of captivity—
sweet and dangerous.
Forgive me when I grow fierce
and understand
when I seek wild mountain meadows.

About the Authors

Space does not allow us to do justice to the biographical statements about the remarkable women contained in this collection. Here are only a few facts about them, mostly related to their writing careers.

LAVONNE J. ADAMS received the 1999 Persephone Poetry Book Publication Award sponsored by the North Carolina Writers Network for her book, *Everyday Still Life*. Her poetry appears in literary journals such as *Karamu, The New Delta Review, The Baltimore Review,* and in *What Have You Lost?,* a poetry anthology for young adults, edited by Naomi Shihab Nye.

LYNN ASCH lives in the Pioneer Valley of western Massachusetts. She is the mother of two daughters, and regards the years of her divorce after twenty-six years of marriage as the most terrifying, most painful, and most healing period in her life.

SHARON LYNN BEAR holds a Ph.D. in Counseling Psychology from the University of Southern California. She is the founder of Bear's Research, Writing & Editing Service, located in Westwood, California. She is a research and writing consultant to and editor for university faculty, thesis and dissertation candidates, and aspiring writers around the world.

SHEILA BENDER's newest collection of poems is *Sustenance: New and Selected Poems*. Her books include *Writing Personal Poetry, A Year in the Life, Journaling for Self-Discovery,* and *Keeping a Journal You Love*. She lives and works in Los Angeles.

DINA BEN-LEV lives in Ormond Beach, Florida. She is the author of three books of poems; the most recent is *Broken Helix* (Mid-List Press), which was awarded the Eric Mathieu King Prize from the Academy of American Poets. Ben-Lev is also the recipient of an NEA (National Endowment for the Arts) fellowship in poetry. She is in the process of completing a spiritual autobiography and is helping several new writers edit their spiritual memoirs.

JANE AHARONI BERMAN, a native New Yorker, has lived in Israel since 1969. She has two married daughters, a son serving in the army, and a baby grandson. Although happily in love and remarried, she still regards her divorce as a defining moment in her life. She lives on Nir Etzion, a religious moshav, and teaches English at a high school in Haifa.

J.B. BERNSTEIN has had writings published in more than 100 journals and anthologies including *The Brownstone Review*, *The Comstock Review*, and *Kalliope*. In 1997, she won second place for her poem in The Lou Daniels Memorial Contest and was nominated for a Pushcart Prize for a short story. She lives in New Haven, Connecticut.

ADRIAN BLEVINS taught for many years at Hollins University. She is the author of *The Man Who Went Out for Cigarettes,* a Bright Hill Press award-winning chapbook, and has published poems and essays in *The Southern Review, The Massachusetts Review, Painted Bride Quarterly* and many other magazines and journals. She is more recently the recipient of the Lamar York Prize for Nonfiction and has published essays in *The Utne Reader,* and *The Chattahoochee Review.*

SUSANNE R. BOWERS was very active in the writing community in Houston until her untimely death in 2000. Her writings appeared in numerous journals, including *Sulphur River Literary Review; Suddenly: Prose Poetry and Sudden Fiction; Rattle; Porcupine Literary Magazine;* and *ArtWord Quarterly*. Her first book of poems, *The Space We Leave Between,* was published by Touchstone Press in 1994.

CELESTE BOWMAN divides her time between a downtown efficiency apartment in Houston and her cabin on fifty acres in the Texas Hill Country. She stays busy with animal rescue, is creating a wildlife refuge on her acreage, and writes in her spare time. Her work has been published in the *Houston Chronicle, Nerve Cowboy, Lilliput,* and *Happy*. Her fiction has been nominated twice for the Pushcart Prize; and she was a finalist in the 1998 PEN Awards in poetry.

JANIE BREGGIN's poems have appeared in many journals, including *Howling, Womankind, The Poetry of Women, Our Journey, Buffalo Bones,* and *How Do I Love Thee*? She has won numerous poetry contests, including first prize for poetry in the Denver Metro Chapter of the National Writers Association 1995 Writing Contest.

JANET I. BUCK's poetry and fiction have appeared in *CrossConnect, The Melic Review, The Pittsburgh Quarterly, Kimera, The Rose & Thorn, 2River View, Southern Ocean Review, Urban Spaghetti, Perihelion, Mind Fire, Born Magazine, Poetry Life & Times, Pif Magazine, Samsara Quarterly, Big Bridge,* and hundreds of journals worldwide. She is a recipient of The H.G. Wells Award for Literary Excellence. Newton's Baby Press published her first collection of poetry, *Calamity's Quilt*.

SUSAN CLAYTON-GOLDNER is a graduate of the University of Arizona's Creative Writing Program. She has published two novels, *Finding a Way Back* and *Just Another Heartbeat,* and her poems have appeared in literary journals and anthologies, including *Hawaii Pacific Best of a Decade, New Millennium Writings, The Westward Review, Animals as Teachers and Healers, Essential Love,* and *Our Mothers Ourselves.*

PAT CRAIG is a writer and career counselor living in Simi Valley, Ca. She is an affiliate of Amherst Writers and Artists and leads a writers' support group called The Writing Community.

BARBARA DANIELS' chapbook, *The Woman Who Tries To Believe,* won the Quentin R. Howard Prize from Wind Publications. Her poems have appeared in *The Massachusetts Review, The Seattle Review, Poet Lore, Slant,* and elsewhere. She has received an Individual Artist Fellowship from the New Jersey State Council on the Arts and completed an MFA in poetry at Vermont College.

BARBARA DECESARE's first book, *jigsaweyesore* (Anti-Man, 1999), has been called "what thunder looks like in writing" by the *Baltimore Sun*. She lives with her three children and is an MFA candidate at Goddard College in Vermont.

KAREN ETHELSDATTAR is cofounder of a women's ritual group, Eve's Well. Her poems have appeared in *WomanSpirit; Off Our Backs; New Women, New Church; Christian Science Monitor;* St. Joan's International Alliance's *The Arc,* and in Starhawk's book, *The Spiral Dance.* Her writings have also appeared in the Papier-Mache Press anthologies, *If I Had My Life To Live Over I Would Pick More Daisies* and *At Our Core: Women Writing About Power.*

MARTHA EVERHART was a finalist for the Bellwether Prize (judged by Barbara Kingsolver), for her first novel, *Beds of Broken Glass*, which also won second prize in the 2001 Mystery/Suspense Novel Contest sponsored by the Writers' League of Texas. Her writing has appeared in *New Texas 2000, A Writer's Choice Literary Journal*, *Suddenly*, and *My Kitchen Table*. A chapbook, *The Fringe: A Nurse's Notes*, was published by *A Writer's Choice Literary Journal* in 1999.

SANDRA GARDNER's poetry has been published in a number of small press magazines, journals, and anthologies. Gardner, a freelance writer living in Woodstock, New York, is a former columnist for *The New Jersey Weekly* section of *The New York Times,* and is the author of four non-fiction books. Two of her novels have been finalists for literary prizes.

FRANCES ISAACS GILMORE, a former industrial hygienist and high-school teacher, is a community organizer and anti-racism teacher in Lowell, Massachusetts. She is a watercolor artist as well as a poet.

LUCINDA GREY teaches creative writing at UNC Charlotte where she edited *Southern Poetry Review* for several years. Her book, *Ribbon Around a Bomb,* won the Quentin R. Howard Poetry Prize and was published in 1994. In 1992 she won the North Carolina Arts Council's Writer's Residency in southern France. Recent work appeared in *Tar River Poetry, Shenandoah,* and *Poet & Critic.*

MARY HAZZARD has written four novels, as well as numerous plays, poems and short stories. A Yale Drama graduate, she has received fellowships from the National Endowment for the Arts, the Provincetown Fine Arts Work Center, Yaddo, and the MacDowell Colony. Her 1999 novel, *Family Blood,* won the Ariadne Fiction Prize. She lives near Boston.

BARBARA HENDRYSON's poetry has appeared in more than sixty literary journals and anthologies, and has recently appeared or is forthcoming in: *Southern Poetry Review*, *Alaska Quarterly Review*, *Berkeley Poetry Review*, *The Sun*, *Montserrat Review*, *Bellingham Review*, *Kalliope*, and others; and in the anthologies, *Cries of the Spirit*, Beacon Press; *Sixteen Voices*, Mariposa Press; *Out of the Dark* and *Hard Love*, Queen of Swords Press; *Essential Love*, Poetworks, and others.

KATHI HENNESSY is a writing tutor, freelance news correspondent, and teacher. She earned a B.A. in English from the University of New Hampshire, and an M.A. in Humanities from California State University. Her poetry has appeared in the *Granite Review, Compass Rose,* the *Anthology of New England Writers,* and *Victory Park,* the journal of the New Hampshire Institute of Art. Her short fiction has appeared in *Vermont Ink* and the 2000 anthology, The *World's Shortest Stories of Love and Death.*

MARY KENNAN HERBERT, a former senior editor in book publishing, now teaches writing and literature courses at colleges in New York City. Her poems have appeared in numerous literary journals, including *The Chattahoochee Review*, *The Arkansas Review*, *Paris/Atlantic*, *Terra Nova*, *The Santa Monica Review*, *Theology Today*, and *Architrave*. Ginninderra Press in Australia published her first three books of poetry, and Meadow Geese Press in Massachusetts published her fourth collection in December, 2000.

FRANCES DOWNING HUNTER teaches English at Arkansas State University. A finalist in The Atlanta Review Poetry 1997 Competition, she received an International Merit Award in the Poetry 1996 Competition. Chiron Review Press published her first full-length poetry collection, *The Sanguine Sunrise*. Her poetry has appeared in *San Fernando Poetry Journal*, *American Tanka*, *Dream International Quarterly*, *The Sierra Nevada College Review*, *Raskolnikov's Cellar*, *Poetry Motel*, *Free Focus*, *Sunstone*, and *Everywhere Is Someplace Else*, a literary anthology.

MYRNA JACKSON's writings have appeared in *California State Quarterly*, *Echoes*, *The Bridge*, *Slant*, *The North Carolina Independent*, *Buffalo Bones*, *Roundtable*, *Excursus*, and in a collection by the William Oster Literary Society. The *North Carolina Independent* named her as one of three winners in their 1996 poetry contest. Jackson holds degrees in English from the University of Pennsylvania, where she taught for several years in the composition program. She is now professionally engaged in library development and outreach for the Duke University libraries.

MARGARET KAUFMAN lives in Marin County, California, where she leads writing workshops. Former editor for *The Western Journal of Medicine*, she currently edits fiction for *The Marlboro Review*. Recipient of a Marin County Artist Grant, Kaufman is also a founding member of 16 Rivers Press, a not-for-profit collective press. Her poetry collection, *Snake at the Wrist*, was published in the spring of 2002.

TINA KELLEY is a reporter for the *Metro* section of *The New York Times*. Her poetry has appeared in *Poetry Northwest*, which recently awarded her its Theodore Roethke prize. Her writings have also been published in *Prairie Schooner*, *Fine Madness*, and *The Journal of the American Medical Association*.

MELISSA PRUNTY KEMP is a college English instructor at Morris Brown College in Atlanta, Georgia. She has instructed composition and literature for twelve years. She is also a freelance professional writer. Kemp is currently experimenting with prose and more unconventional poetry forms.

ANN B. KNOX has published two books of poetry: *Staying Is Nowhere* (winner of SCOP-Writer's Center 1996) and *Stonecrop* (winner of the Washington Writers Publishing House Prize). Her poems have appeared in many literary journals, including *Poetry*, *Nimrod,* and *Alaska Review*. For eighteen years she has been an editor of *Antietam Review*. A collection of her short stories, *Late Summer Break*, was published in 1997 by Papier-Mache Press.

JOYCE LA MERS, a Montana native, lives in Oxnard, California. Her poetry has appeared widely in national publications including *Light Quarterly, The Formalist,* and *Solo*. Her chapbook, *Grandma Rationalizes an Enthusiasm for Skydiving,* was a 1996 publication from Mille Grazie Press.

PATRICIA LANTAY is a recent recipient of the Richard Hugo Poetry Award sponsored by *Amelia Magazine*. In 1998, she received Second Prize in the Grand Prize Award from the National Federation of State Poetry Societies. Her writings have appeared in *Alkali Flats, The Lucid Stone, Elk River Review, Poetry Motel, The TMP Irregular, Liberty Hill Review, Hodge Podge Poetry, Encore, Ohio Poetry Day Anthologies, The Best of 1996, The Best of 1998, The Best of 1999,* and the *West Virginia Poetry Society Anthology of 1994*. She is editor and publisher of *The Forum Column,* a newsletter representing The New York Poetry Forum.

VEVA DIANNE LAWSON is a playwright, fiction writer, poet, and attorney. Her writings have appeared in *Waterways, The Old Red Kimono, ArtWord Quarterly* and in the anthology, *Suddenly II*. Her plays, *Broken Things* and *The Services of Women,* were produced in Houston at Stages Theater as part of Edward Albee's play production workshops. Lawson won the Howard Moss Poetry Prize in1997 and was a finalist in the Eugene O'Neill National Playwright's Conference in 2000.

STELLASUE LEE's writing has appeared in *Crossing the Double Yellow Line; After I Fall,* a collection of four Los Angeles poets; *Over To You,* an exchange of poems with David Widup; and *13 Los Angeles Poets,* the *ONTHEBUS* Poets Series Number One (Bombshelter Press).

P.M. LOVETT is the daughter of a wonderful mother, mother of two delightful sons, teacher of elementary age children, and a lover of the sun, gardens, seashore, books, and laughter.

ANNE LUSBY-DENHAM's poems have been published in *Bohemian Bridge, The Potomac Guardian, The Shepherdstown Chronicle, The Public Pamphlet,* and *Shenandoah Poets*, an anthology. Composer Lawrence Moss of the University of Maryland set several of her poems to music in the dance-drama, *Dreamscape*. Her poetry has also been included in *Public Hanging,* a gallery show combining art and poetry. She currently lives in Houston, Texas.

DIANE LUTOVICH is a past co-president of the Marin Poetry Center and currently a vice-president of California Poets in the Schools. Her writings have been published in many journals, including *The Lucid Stone* and *Beside the Sleeping Maiden*. Recently, a non-fiction book, *Nobody's Child: How Older Women Say Good-bye to Their Mothers,* was published by Baywood Publishing.

LESLIE LYTLE is a farmer and writer who lives in rural Tennessee. She was named Farmer of the Year by the Franklin County Soil Conservation District. Her writing life thrives, as well. Her stories and poems have appeared in *Carolina*

Quarterly, The Georgia Review, Graham House Review, The Literary Review, New England Review and Bread Loaf Quarterly, Poet Lore, Thoroughbred Times, The Chattahoochee Review, and *Zone Three.*

AMANDA MACLEOD is a writer and dance instructor living in Los Angeles. When not writing, dancing, or caring for her two daughters, she is teaching herself to play the Gaelic harp.

LINDA MALNACK's poetry has appeared in many journals, including *America, The Amherst Review, Calyx, The Seattle Review,* and *Southern Humanities Review,* and she has published a chapbook titled *Bone Beads* (Paper Boat Press, 1997).

ARLENE L. MANDELL's poetry and short stories have appeared in more than a hundred publications, including *Art/Life*, *Paterson Literary Review*, *Pegasus Review,* and *The New York Times* "Metropolitan Diary." Her work has also been published in six anthologies. A poem, "Little Girl Grown," which originally appeared in "Metropolitan Diary," was recently published in *Mothers and Daughters: A Poetry Celebration,* edited by June Cotner and published by Random House.

JOANNE MCCARTHY taught English and creative writing at Tacoma Community College for many years. Her poems appear in literary magazines and anthologies including At *Our Core: Women Writing About Power* and *I Am Becoming the Woman I've Wanted* (Papier-Mache Press 1998, 1994); *Claiming the Spirit Within* (Beacon Press 1996); and in her book, *Shadowlight* (Broken Moon Press 1989).

REBECCA MCCLANAHAN's fourth volume of poetry is *Naked as Eve* (Copper Beech Press, 2000). She has also published *Word Painting: A Guide to Writing More Descriptively* (Writer's Digest Books, 1999), which has recently been released in paperback. McClanahan's *Write Your Heart Out* was recently published by Walking Stick Press, and her book of essays is forthcoming from University of Georgia Press.

MARGUERITE MCKIRGAN recently moved to the St. Louis area and is currently rediscovering the beauty and the pleasures of living in the Midwest. She has connected with a writers group and is beginning to write again after a five-year hiatus.

DODIE MESSER MEEKS worked on the *Galveston Tribune* and the *Galveston Daily News* and covered Galveston for the *Houston Chronicle* in the sixties. Her poems have appeared in *The Anthology of Magazine Verse* and *Yearbook of American Poetry*; *Architrave*; *Visions International*; *The Unitarian-Universalist Anthology*; *McCall's*; *The Southwest Review*; *Voices International*; *The Pudding House Anthology*; and a couple of hundred other literary publications.

ELISABETH MURAWSKI's first book, *Moon and Mercury*, was published in 1990 by Washington Writers' Publishing House. A chapbook, *Troubled By an Angel*, was published in 1997 by Cleveland State University Poetry Center. Her numerous journal publications include: *The New Republic*, *Grand Street*, *American Poetry Review*, *Crazyhorse*, *Doubletake*, *Poetry Northwest*, *Virginia Quarterly Review*, *Shenandoah*, *Quarterly West*, *Field*, *Ohio Review*, *The Journal*, *The Literary Review*, *Cumberland Poetry Review*, *Puerto del Sol*, and *Carolina Quarterly*.

SUSAN R. NORTON has been widely published in more than seventy literary journals, magazines, anthologies, newspapers and greeting cards. Her work has appeared in such publications as: *The Southern Poetry Review, Writer's World Magazine, Silver Quill, The Knews*, and Norton has been the recipient of seven awards in writing.

MARY E. O'DELL is head of Green River Writers, Inc., a seventeen-year-old, Louisville-based organization, which offers feedback and support for writers of every level. O'Dell's latest poetry collection, *Poems for Man Who Weighs Light,* is available from Edwin Mellen Press, Lewiston, New York. O'Dell's short fiction has been published in such places as *Glimmer Train* and *The American Voice*.

KEDDY ANN OUTLAW, once a potter and subsistence farmer living in upstate New York, now lives in Houston as a writer and public librarian. Her poems have appeared in *Borderlands: Texas Poetry Review, Grasslands Review, Sulphur River Review, The Texas Poetry Calendar, Lilliput Review,* and several anthologies published by Papier-Mache Press. Her short stories have been anthologized in *Texas Short Stories* (1997) and *Texas Short Stories II* (2000), published by Browder Springs Press.

JUNE OWENS resides in Central Florida. Originally trained as a classical singer, her poems, book reviews, and nonfiction have appeared in *Atlanta Review*; *The Caribbean Writer*; *Manoa*; *Nimrod*; *Quarterly West*; *Snowy Egret*; *Spillway*; *Tirra Lirra* (Australia), and in numerous anthologies, including *The Muse Strikes Back: A Poetic Response by Women to Men* (Story Line Press, 1998); *Essential Love* (Poetworks/Grayson Books, 2000); *GRRRRR: A Collection of Poems About Bears* (Arctos Press, 1999). Owens is the recipient of many poetry awards, among them a Prospect Press First Poetry Book Award for her 1999 collection, *Tree Line*.

MARGE PIERCY, poet, novelist, and essayist, was born in Detroit in 1936. Among her many books of poetry are *Early Grrrl: The Early Poems of Marge Piercy*; *The Art of Blessing the Day: Poems With a Jewish Theme*; *What Are Big Girls Made Of?*; *The Moon Is Always Female*; *Stone, Paper, Knife;* and *Circles on the Water: Selected Poems of Marge Piercy*.

DIANE PINKLEY was born in Missouri, went to college and graduate school in the North, and then spent twenty years in Europe. She is currently a faculty member in the TESOL (Teaching English to Speakers of Other Languages) Program, Department of Arts and Humanities at Teachers College, Columbia University in New York City. She is the author of several textbooks, a few short stories, and many poems.

ELISAVIETTA RITCHIE won the Anamnesis Press Competition for her poetry book, *Awaiting Permission to Land: Poems 1997-2001*, due 2002. Her short story collection, *In Haste I Write You This Note: Stories & Half-Stories* was a winner in the Washington Writers' Publishing House's premiere fiction competition, (2000). Among her poetry collections are: *The Arc of the Storm; Elegy for the Other Woman: New and Selected Terribly Female Poems; Tightening the Circle Over Eel Country; Raking the Snow*; and chapbooks *Wild Garlic: The Journal of Maria* X; and *A Wound-Up Cat and Other Bedtime Stories*. She edited *The Dolphin's Arc: Endangered Creatures of the Sea*.

LINDA GOODMAN ROBINER's chapbook, *Reverse Fairy Tale,* was published by Pudding House Publications. More than 200 of her poems have appeared in such magazines as *The William and Mary Review, The Chattahoochee Review, North Atlantic Review, Chiron Review, The Neovictorian, Potomac Review*, and in anthologies, such as *The Practice of Peace; Heal Your Soul, Heal the World;* and *A Contemporary American Survey*.

TANIA ROCHELLE lives in Marietta, Georgia. Her work has appeared in a variety of print and online journals, including *Iris, Snake Nation, New York Quarterly,* and *Blue Moon Review*. A regular contributor and columnist for the webzine *Waysouth*, she teaches writing at the Portfolio Center in Atlanta.

JANE BUTKIN ROTH lives in the Houston area. Her writings have appeared in more than seventy publications, including the *Houston Chronicle, Oklahoma Today, Windsor Review, Poet's Market 1999, Jewish Women's Literary Annual,* and *The Journal of Poetry Therapy*. Her poems were recently published in the anthologies, *Mothers and Daughters: A Poetry Celebration* (Random House); *Haiku-Sine* (Lazywood Press); *Essential Love* (Grayson Books); and *Suddenly: Prose Poetry and Sudden Fiction* (Stone River Press).

DEBORAH MILLER ROTHSCHILD lives in Houston, Texas, and is a freelance writer and former staff writer for the *Sacramento Union*. Her recent work has appeared in *Suddenly*, the *Houston Chronicle, It's Great To Have a Sister Like You, Blue Mountain Arts,* and *Inside Service Corporation International*. She is communication and development director for Texans for Gun Safety, a grassroots non-profit organization that reduces gun violence through education and public policy.

MARY KOLADA SCOTT wrote a weekly poetry column for the *Ventura County Star* for four years. Her poems, short stories, articles and photographs have been published in more than 70 magazines, newspapers and anthologies. Currently, her work appears in three new poetry collections: *Essential Love, Split Verse*, and *Touched by Adoption*.

JOAN JOBE SMITH has been a go-go dancer, law student, MFA grad student, creative writing teacher, editor/publisher, and poet. Her work has appeared extensively in literary journals in the U.S., U.K, Ireland, Sweden, Mexico, and Germany. Her collection of "go-go girl poems" is called *Jehovah Jukebox* and was published in 1993. Smith is working on a second collection, *In the Raw*. Her memoirs are titled *Tales of an Ancient Go-Go Girl.* Her chapbook, *Picking the Lock on the Door to Paradise*, won second prize in the Nerve Cowboy Chapbook Contest 2000.

LAUREL SPEER's latest publication is a poem pamphlet titled *Sweet Jesus in the Afternoon*. Her poetry has appeared in numerous publications, including *Chiron Review, Santa Barbara Review, Descant, Sulphur River Literary Review, Suddenly, Pearl, Grasslands Review, Santa Clara Review, The Paterson Literary Review,* and *Timber Creek Review.* Speer is a contributing editor for *Small Press Review.*

MAGI STONE presents an interactive poetry workshop called *Imagine That!* She is a staff member of the Florida Suncoast Writers' Conference. She has been Poet Laureate of Hollywood, Florida since 1994. She is past vice president and now a board member of the Hannah Kahn Poetry Foundation. Her chapbook, *Pieces of Glass* (poems about women), was published in 1994.

ROSE MARY SULLIVAN's poetry and prose have appeared in hundreds of publications throughout the U.S. and Canada, including *Earth's Daughters, Bitterroot, International Poetry Journal, California Quarterly, Connecticut Writer, Mediphors, Passager, Potato Eyes, Kalliope, Threads of Experience* (Papier-Mache Press), *The Potomac Review*, and *The South Dakota Review*. She has won numerous poetry awards. Sullivan was one of the top ten finalists in the country in the Jeannette Gould Maino Poetry Awards Contest sponsored by the National League of American PEN Women.

PATTI TANA is Professor of English at Nassau Community College (SUNY) and Associate Editor of the *Long Island Quarterly*. Her poetry books include *When the Light Falls Short of the Dream* (Eighth Moon Press), *Wetlands* (Papier-Mache Press) and *Ask the Dreamer Where Night Begins* (Kendall/Hunt). Her poems have appeared in *When I Am an Old Woman I Shall Wear Purple* (Papier-Mache Press), *Hiram Poetry Review, Long Island Poetry Review, Anthology of Magazine Verse*, and the *Nassau Review*.

DIANALEE VELIE has a Master of Arts in Writing from Manhattanville College. She has served as faculty advisor of *Inkwell* Magazine, the literary journal of Manhattanville College's MAW program, where she has taught The Craft of Writing. Velie has also taught poetry, memoir and short story writing at Norwalk Community College, poetry at the State University of New York in Purchase and English Composition at the University of Connecticut at Stamford.

TAMMY VITALE is a 50-something young crone who has begun to wear purple, write poetry, and get published. She has been a guest on Grace Cavalieri's WPFW89.3FM's "The Poet and the Poem" program in Washington D.C. She received her Master's in Story and Social Change from Goddard.

NANCY LYNCH WEISS lives in eastern Pennsylvania, where she works full time in a group home for troubled boys. She uses her poetry and drama in the therapy work she does with abused women and children. Nancy's poetry has been published in several poetry magazines and anthologies.

HENNY WENKART originated and edited an anthology, *Sarah's Daughters Sing* (1990) and the *Jewish Women's Literary Annual*. She also originated and coedited the anthology *Which Lilith?* (Jason Aronson 1998) and translated *Memoirs of a Grandmother* by the nineteenth-century writer, Pauline Wengeroff. Wenkart's poems have appeared in numerous literary journals, including *Prairie Schooner, Confrontation*, and *Paterson Literary Review*, and in a number of anthologies.

ANNE WILSON wrote the poems included in this anthology in 1996. Since then, she has published hundreds of poems in journals and anthologies, among them: *Bitter Oleander; South Dakota Review; Rattle; New Millennium Writings; Weber Studies; The Owen Wister Review; Green Hills Literary Lantern;* and *Phoebe: Journal of Feminist Aesthetics*. She has won nearly thirty awards and teaches poetry at the University of California San Diego.

FRANCINE WITTE taught English and Creative Writing in the New York City public high schools for eight years. She is a poet, fiction writer, screenwriter, and playwright. Owl Creek Press published her chapbook, *Magic in the Streets*, in 1994.

LEILANI WRIGHT lives in Mesa, Arizona. Her poems and essays have appeared in *Calyx, Tampa Review, Hayden's Ferry Review, Indiana Review,* and *Poets & Writers,* among other journals. She is primary editor of *Fever Dreams: Contemporary Arizona Poetry* (University of Arizona Press, 1997) and author of the chapbook, *A Natural Good Shot* (White Eagle Coffee Store Press, 1994). Wright presently works at the Arizona Commission on the Arts.

NANCY MEANS WRIGHT has published nine books; the most recent is a mystery novel, *Poison Apples* (St. Martin's Press, 2000). Other works include two mainstream novels and two non-fiction books. Her poems have appeared in *Carolina Quarterly, Wisconsin Review, Bellingham Review,* and elsewhere; in anthologies from Beacon Press, St. Martin's, Ashland Poetry Review, and elsewhere; and in two chapbooks—most recently, *Walking Up Into the Volcano* (Pudding House Publications, 2000).

ANDRENA ZAWINSKI, whose work has appeared in *Quarterly West, Paterson Literary Review, Rattle, Santa Clara Review, Nimrod,* and others, is a Pittsburgh born-and-raised poet living in the San Francisco Bay Area. Her collection, *Traveling in Reflected Light*, was released by Pig Iron Press as a Kenneth Patchen Competition winner. She is feature editor at http://www.poetrymagazine.com.

Grateful acknowledgment is made to the authors, editors, and publishers of the journals and books where the following poems first appeared:

Lavonne J. Adams, "The Math of Marriage," *Everyday Still Life* (North Carolina Writers Network).

Sheila Bender, "After We Collected Treasures From the Beach and Forests," *Love From the Coastal Route* (Duckabush Press).

Dina Ben-Lev, "Driving," *Field;* "In Sweetness and in Light," *Sou'wester;* "How It Was," *Slipstream;* "Home on New Year's," *Salt Hill Journal*.

J.B. Bernstein, "Tanglewood," *Kalliope: A Journal of Women's Literature and Art*.

Adrian Blevins, "The Inheritance" and "The Wilderness You Know Best," *The Man Who Went Out for Cigarettes* (Bright Hill Press).

Celeste Bowman, "Rituals," *Sink Full of Dishes*.

Janet I. Buck, "Popped Umbrellas," *PoetryRepairShop*.

Barbara Daniels, "Mark on a Mirror," *The Woman Who Tries To Believe* (Wind Publications); "Finding the Way Out," *Laurel Review*.

Barbara DeCesare, "A Truth Like Blood," *The Pearl*.

Karen Ethelsdattar, "The First Time I Married," *If I Had My Life To Live Over I Would Pick More Daisies* (Papier-Mache Press).

Sandra Gardner, "Love Story," *Trust* (Outloud Press).

Frances Isaacs Gilmore, "Provincetown Hook," *Buffalo Bones*.

Mary Hazzard, "Untrue," *Dark Horse*.

Barbara Hendryson, "Prayer for a Tenspeed Heart," *Cries of the Spirit* (Beacon Press).

Kathi Hennessy, "Semantics," *Feelings: A Journal of Poetic Thought and Verse*.

Mary Kennan Herbert, "August Alarums," *Long Island Quarterly;* "At a Family Reunion," *The Mind's Eye*; "A Beautiful Bowl," *Architrave*.

Frances Downing Hunter, "Turbulence," *The Sanguine Sunrise* (Chiron Review Press).

Margaret Kaufman, "Waking," *Gods and Mortals: Modern Poems on Classical Myths;* "The New Kitchen," *Girasole*.

Ann B. Knox, "*I Divorce You*," *New York Quarterly;* "Clematis," *Ohio Poetry Review.*

Patricia Lantay, "No Earthly Paradise," *Elk River Review*.

Stellasue Lee, "Report," *Sheila-Na-Gig;* "My Name Is Stellasue," *Spillway*.

Anne Lusby-Denham, "After the Divorce," *The Public Pamphlet*.

Diane Lutovich, "0 Into 0," *The Lucid Stone;* "Hatted," *Staple*.

Linda Malnack, "Tell Them," *Verve*.

Arlene L. Mandell, "Bridal Veil," *Millennium Vintage 2000: Poets of the Vineyard Anthology*.

Joanne McCarthy, "The Lover Returns," *In a Nutshell;* "Sea Change," *Portraits*.

Dodie Messer Meeks, "Advice to a Bride," *Modern Maturity*.

Elisabeth Murawski, "The Audience," *Willow Springs*.

Marge Piercy, "Never-never," *Circles on the Water* (Alfred A. Knopf/Random House); "A story wet as tears," *Stone, Paper, Knife* (Alfred A. Knopf/Random House).

Elisavietta Ritchie, "Elegy for the Other Woman," *New York Quarterly*. "Clearing the Path," *When I Am an Old Woman I Shall Wear Purple* (Papier-Mache Press); "After Long Absence, Mail Call" and "Savings and Thrift," *The New York Times*.

Tania Rochelle, "Feeding the Worms," *Split Verse: Poems To Heal Your Heart* (Midmarch Arts Press, 2000).

Jane Butkin Roth, "Breaking Bread," *Owen Wister Review*; "Faulty Design," *Apples and Oranges, Oranges and Apples*.

Joan Jobe Smith, "Picking the Lock on the Door to Paradise," *Picking the Lock on the Door to Paradise* (Liquid Paper Press).

Laurel Speer, "Things We Do Not Talk Of," *Cookies* (Geryon Press); "Candyman," *Art/Life*.

Patti Tana, "The Last Tear" and "The Words," *Ask the Dreamer Where Night Begins* (Kendall/Hunt Publishing Company).

Tammy Vitale, "Changes," *Potomac Review*.

Henny Wenkart, "On Waking From a Nap," *lips* magazine; "Comfort," *Paterson Literary Review*.

Francine Witte, "Falling," *Bellingham Review*; "Perception," *Green Mountains Review*; "Mother-in-Law," *Calliope*.

Nancy Means Wright, "Acrophobia," *Sojourner;* "Hunger," *VOX*.

Andrena Zawinski, "Trying To Raise the Dead," *Santa Clara Review*; "Some Women, Take Heart," *The Pittsburgh Quarterly*.